EMPATH SURVIVAL GUIDE: HOW TO MAKE YOUR PERSONALITY A SUPERPOWER

Embrace The Gift of Empathy, Learn How to Protect Yourself From Narcissistic Relationships and Welcome Your Happiest Self

Table of Contents

Introduction 5

Chapter One - Are You an Empath? 9
What is an Empath? 9
10 Signs You're An Empath 10
Empathic, Introverted and Sensitive: What is the Difference? 13
8 Misconceptions About Empaths 15

Chapter Two - Understanding the Empath Gift 18
The Science Behind Empathy and Empaths 19

Chapter Three - The Empath Reality 32
5 Bad Habits that Empaths Must Let Go 34
The 5 Common Health Problems of Empaths 35

Chapter Four - The Injured Empath 39
What is Compassion Fatigue? 41
Signs of an Injured Empath 44
Beware: The Victim Complex 46
The Truth About Empaths and Addiction 48

Chapter Five - The Dangers of Being an Empath 51
Why Narcissists Are Drawn to Empaths 54
Why Empaths are Drawn to Narcissists 55
Signs an Empath is with an Emotional Vampire 56

Chapter Six - Healing the Empath Heart 61
5 Healing Activities for Empaths to Relax 61
Powerful Techniques for Healing and Self-Protection 66
Positive Affirmations All Empaths Must Know 68

Chapter Seven - The Healthy, Happy Empath 70
The 5 Powerful Lessons Every Empath Must Learn 70
Daily Practices of a Healthy Empath 72
Stop Empathizing with Pain and Start Empathizing with Joy 75

Chapter Eight - Empathy as a Superpower 78
The 7 Natural Gifts that All Empaths Possess 78

The Best Jobs for Empaths 80
Conclusion **86**

Introduction

There is a unique breed of individuals who are gifted with the ability to not only experience their emotions and those of the people around them; they can also experience the physical pain of other people. These individuals walk into a room and within minutes, they can accurately pick on the vibes of the people in the room. This may sound like a cool superpower that belongs on the set of X-Men but in reality, it is something that can be very difficult to deal with and not many people are emotionally and mentally equipped to manage these gifts. You may identify such persons as people who are overly sensitive. Psychology experts profile them as empaths and their story is not always one of those happily ever after types.

For the longest time, emotions have been frowned on as a weakness and displaying them was described as a feminine trait at best. In worst-case scenarios, people who showed their emotions one too many times were regarded as persons who have no control over how they feel. Derogatory terms like "unpredictable", "walking eggshells", "cry baby" and so many other names that are not fit to print are used to tag people who dare to show their emotions. The general negative perception about emotions has woven itself into the very foundation of the society which is the family. There are a lot of families today who enforce strict measures to deter any display of emotions at home. This need to shut down a very crucial aspect of one's self has led many to suffer silently for a better part of their lives. For an empath, they live with the double trauma of dealing with their own emotions as well as the pain of others. This leaves them constantly emotionally overwhelmed. If you picked up this book, chances are you are an empath or you know an empath who struggles with their emotional burden.

But, what if I told you that those very emotions that you feel cripple you and your ability to thrive can be channeled into making you a better version of yourself and in so doing, you can enrich your life? Sounds too good to be true right? Well, here is one truth that many of us heard but don't really believe because they have been dumped in the same category as those ineffective life clichés people dish out. Your emotions are anything but weak. In fact, it is described as one of the most powerful forces possessed by humans and before we go any further in this book, I can tell you that shutting your emotions down is not going to do you any good. The only way forward is to embrace those feelings by choosing to accept your abilities as an empath.

Being an empath goes beyond understanding your emotions. As an empath, you embrace the emotions of others. The wealth of understanding you acquire in this process gifts you with a unique perspective of the world and the people that you encounter daily. This goes a long way to help you foster relationships that are more meaningful and impactful. Most importantly, as an empath, you develop a deeper connection with yourself that truly empowers you to understand pain. This is not some new-age psychobabble fad that is trending at the moment. This is you taking back the power from people who have tagged the way you truly feel as weak and evolving into the "real you" that you are meant to be.

With this book, you can finally take off the mask you have been forced to wear by the society and step into your reality. As an empath who had to navigate the process of my "becoming" without a guide, I know how difficult to make sense of how you feel. I spent lots of hours daily scouring through the internet for information on these rainbows of emotions that I go through every day. I have come close to several breakdowns not because I had a lot of bad experiences or that I was taking on more workload than I normally would. I was just constantly overwhelmed by what I was feeling. People would come to me with their problems because I had a knack for being such a great listener and I could connect with them in ways that they found comforting. However, I also ended up having to deal with the emotional aftermath of their predicaments. I sought counseling and for a while, that helped me. But, I still sought validation from the people I deal with on a day to day basis. I didn't want to crumble emotionally in front of them so that I could keep being their go-to counselor.

This meant I had to act like I had my life together 100% of the time even if in reality, it felt like I could barely keep the seams from falling apart. In very succinct terms, I was a mess. With the contents of this book, I was able to;

- Make sense of the emotions I was feeling
- Find the strength to embrace these seemingly chaotic parts of myself
- Learn to manage my emotions better
- Unlock my natural intuitive nature and pay more attention to my instincts
- Become better at managing my relationships with people

Maybe you are reading my story and feeling like you are looking into the mirror of your own life. Here is an assurance, if I can find my way back, so can you. However, there is a caveat. Living as an empath requires you being deliberate about your decisions. Anything less could send you on a downward spiral to a dark place that not many people recover from. Before you flip over to the next chapter, I want you to take a moment and decide right here, right now that you are going to be more deliberate about the choices that you make going forward.

That said, the information you would receive in this book are practical steps you can take daily to help you better manage your emotions while navigating the murky emotional waters of other people. At the end of this book, you should be able to stand on a rooftop and proudly declare that you know who you are. That knowledge is powerful and very uplifting. So, to begin the next chapter of your life, turn over to the next page. Things are about to get exciting.

Chapter One - Are You an Empath?

I was a teenager when I had my first encounter with the word "empath." It was from a television series that was popular at the time. In this series, the empath was portrayed as someone who was gifted with divine powers and the ability to feel everything the people around them felt. This empath could feel their pain, their joy, their anger, and even their fears. In this fictional world, the powers of the empath were transferable but if anyone other than a true empath attempted to take these powers, they would be crushed by the weight of the emotions they were forced to experience. This interpretation of an empath is certainly fascinating but it is also very extreme.

Sci-fi lovers share a similar view with the creators of this fantasy series. Culturally, empaths are believed to be humans who possess this paranormal ability to accurately sense the emotional state of others. A popular empath in today's sci-fi trend would be Mantis from the movie, *Guardians of the Galaxy*. Again, this is all very cool but reality tells us a different story.

What is an Empath?

An empath is simply a person with a heightened awareness of the emotions around them. Beyond this awareness, empaths tend to show a lot of empathy towards other people – so much they can experience the emotions of others as if they were their own. Empaths don't just observe people; they have the innate ability to experience them from the inside. The term "ability" is used loosely here. It does not connote the existence of supernatural traits, rather it is directed at a personality trait that uniquely defines them.

In psychology, empaths are described as people who have a great amount of empathy for others. Given everything I've explained so far, it might feel a little disappointing to see empaths defined with such simplicity. Empaths are powerfully unique because they can sense emotions that the people around them try to hide. Without the right information, however, this "uniqueness" can cause a lot of frustration. That said, how can you tell if you are truly an empath and not simply projecting what you hope you are?

I have compiled a list that explores the characteristics of most empaths. If you relate to six or more of the following traits, you are likely an empath.

10 Signs You're An Empath

1. Crowded spaces cause you to feel overwhelmed

When you are in a sea of people, their emotions wash over you like waves and for a person who has a tendency to feel everything, it can leave you feeling overwhelmed. The sensation is akin to experiencing sensory overload where all of your senses are firing off in different directions.

2. You personalize the experiences of others

When a friend comes to you with stories that have strong emotional content, you don't just listen and try to gauge their current state of mind. You see yourself walking in their shoes and reliving their experiences as if they happened to you. At the end of that conversation, you are not just an observer but an active participator in the event. This leaves you just as emotionally riled up as the person who shared their experience with you.

3. You are labeled as "emotional" or "too sensitive"

The way people describe you can give a little insight into your personality. Again, it is not often accurate but it speaks to the actions carried out by you that lead to the general perception of you as any being either too emotional or too sensitive. Now being emotional goes beyond the ability to cry at the drop of the hat. It infers that you get riled up easily.

4. Dealing with people leaves you feeling exhausted

There are people who go through an entire rainbow of emotions in a matter of minutes and these kinds of people can be exhausting to deal with even for the regular person. For an empath, it is twice as bad. You might speak with the mildest mannered person and still get exhausted. Why? Because you can sense the genuine emotions underneath the polite façade. Empaths have a strong radar for someone's true feelings, and they are rarely fooled by pretenses.

5. Most people feel understood by you

This one is a no brainer because you actually understand people. Your ability to see things from their perspective and empathize with them gives you a unique connection to them. In a weird but commendable way, you have this "you are them" bond that puts you in their shoes. For this reason, people tend to be drawn to you. They may feel seen in ways they don't normally feel seen. Sadly, not many people understand empaths, except for other empaths.

6. You are mostly an introvert

Your need to deal with people in very limited doses puts you on the outside of social events, but you likely don't mind it that much. You may even take pleasure in it. Empaths are more likely to be introverted because absorbing the emotions of others can get exhausting, so they tend to need a lot of alone time. Extroverted empaths do exist, but they are rare.

7. You can intuitively sense emotions

This is a big indicator that you are an empath. You are hardly ever fooled by the exterior charms and smiling façade. And if a person makes the mistake of coming to you with lies, you can detect it in a heartbeat without even having to ask questions. There is no technique to this when it comes to you. You are not looking out for that elevated pulse, dilated pupils, or sweaty palms. An empath just knows.

8. You feel connected to nature

This is another general human trait. It is not definitive but it is very common with empaths. Your connection to nature goes beyond the love of trees and sounds of chirping birds. These things give you pleasure but they also give you a sense of rejuvenation. Some people feel replenished after a good night's rest, some seek solace in food but for you, nature is what gets your juices up and flowing.

9. You can never say no to a person in need

Your experiences of other people's pain, suffering or joy does not end with you "feeling" what they feel. It compels you to act. You are not going to leave that little girl crying in the corner simply because her mom is there with her. You want to help make her feel better. Dropping a few coins in the cup for that homeless man is not going to cut it for you. You go home, grab a nice pair of socks, a warm and lovingly used blanket and hand it to him. And if that man stops coming to the area, you might be one of the first to notice. Because empaths have a hard time saying no, many of them struggle with taking on more than they can handle. They want to help everyone, and this can leave them feeling drained.

10. You can empathize with nearly everyone

It's not just about feeling the emotions of homeless people and crying children. Let's face it, it's easy to empathize with the vulnerable people in our society, and any kind person would. Empaths can feel empathy for basically everyone. If two people get in a fight, an empath may not agree with the actions of the aggressor, but they can still have empathy for them. They are able to pinpoint the feelings that caused the person to behave that way and they can empathize with that deep need. A true sign of an empath is when they can emotionally connect with someone that everyone else has turned away from.

Before you started this book, you likely already suspected you were an empath. Now that you've affirmed this, how does it feel? I remember how relieved I felt to finally discover the concept of an empath. It can be a liberating experience to finally identify with something, and to know you're not alone.

Now, let's clear up something important. There are a few words that are used interchangeably with the word "empath.' They may have been used to describe certain aspects of an empath but they do not in any way mean that a person who possesses these qualities is an empath. It is important to provide a clear distinction so as to avoid confusion going forward.

Empathic, Introverted and Sensitive: What is the Difference?

Let us start with the standard dictionary definition of these words before we explore it in depth. A person who is described as empathic essentially shows the ability to understand and share the feelings of another person. An introvert, on the other hand, is a shy and reclusive person who feels more energized when they spend time with themselves. And finally, a sensitive person is someone who is quick to react to the actions or reactions of others. As we can see, these are three different traits with three different meanings. While it is quite possible for a true empath to possess each of these three traits, none of these traits alone can make you an empath.

There are people who have the ability to empathize with others. They feel bad for the pain another person is going through but that does not make them all empaths. Empathy is a wonderful human trait that can give birth to kindness. Empaths, on the other hand, don't just feel bad about the pain of others, they personalize it and make it their own. It takes skillful discipline for an empath to get to a place where their interpretation of the pain of others does not cripple them emotionally.

Some empaths become introverted because they want to hide away from the distress that frequent interactions with people cause them. However, they need those interactions with people to fully make use of their empathic abilities. If they continue to hide away in solitude, that empathic nature may become buried and they'll simply become introverts. Now introverts actually derive pleasure in being alone. Beyond the basic necessity of human interaction (and even then, with very limited people), the introvert takes no pleasure in engaging with people outside of those they have a bond with. For empaths, this solitude is meant to provide a brief reprieve from the onslaught of emotions that hits them during social interactions.

Finally, being sensitive does not immediately translate to a hyper-awareness of the emotions of other people. In fact, in many cases, it can speak to a heightened awareness of only the self. Sensitive people can be acutely aware of their wants and needs, or at the very least, when they're not getting what they want and need. They have a fixed perception of what they feel is right or wrong and when words, actions or perceived reactions go against this information they have of themselves, they react. Even when they react to information affecting others, it is usually centered on their perception of the experiences of others. Many arrogant and narcissistic individuals can be accurately described as sensitive, and they are the opposite of an empath. Ever seen a narcissist get emotional because they aren't getting their way? Exactly. Many narcissists may even call themselves empaths as a way to excuse their inappropriate emotions, but never forget, a true empath must have empathy for other people.

In summary, these can be wonderful traits to have as a person and depending on your personality type, they can serve you well. However, there is more to being an empath than this. Generally speaking, the misuse of certain words to identify an empath are not the only misconceptions out there.

8 Misconceptions About Empaths

1. Empaths are weak

This is just one of the many derogatory labels used by people who do not understand the compassion of an empath. These people look down on any display of emotion other than anger. In reality, empaths can be some of the strongest people you'll ever meet. It can be exhausting to feel so many emotions so easily, and it takes true strength to rise again after feeling so overwhelmed.

2. Empaths cannot be leaders

An organization where there is no form of empathy in management would result in a toxic environment where workers cannot thrive, and they may eventually abandon their posts. An empathic leader is not constantly overflowing with emotions; an empathic leader can simply see his or her employees as human beings, and not just cogs in their machines. Leaders who can empathize with their employees will be more liked by those employees. And when workers in an organization have mutual respect for one another, that organization instantly becomes a fantastic team.

3. Empaths cannot be rational

I believe this is the biggest misconception of them all. An empath is someone who has more than just the facts when they conduct their analyses. Their ability to combine facts with the knowledge they draw from their emotional well gives them a more complete picture of the situation at hand. An empath is not bogged down by emotions in their decision-making, they simply have more information to act on. Empaths may take longer to make a decision, since they have more to consider, but empathy does not impede someone's sense of rationality.

4. Empaths are psychic

This is one of those myths that I wish we didn't have to dispel. Given the accuracy with which an empath can decipher true emotions and catch a liar mid-act, you have to wonder if there is some supernatural angle to it. There's nothing supernatural about it. Empaths are just very skilled at reading microexpressions, tone, and body language. They don't pick up these emotions out of nowhere, the signs are there all along; it's just that most people can't read them.

5. All empaths are introverts

The fact is, most empaths display some introverted tendencies but they are not always introverts. There are plenty of empaths who are extroverts, and many of them are better at hiding it when they feel emotionally overwhelmed. They still need time to recharge and reboot after social scenarios, but they feel more compelled to get back out there once they've had the rest they need.

6. Empaths are fictional characters made up by comic books

I want to launch into a litany of words to disprove this but the fact that you and I exist is enough to show this is not true. Psychologists have publicly acknowledged that empaths do exist and they can even identify what makes us the way we are. Do we need more evidence than that?

7. Empaths are always crying and over-emotional

Most people expect an empath to have an emotional meltdown every hour or so. Our abilities as empaths allow us to access a doorway that not many people can reach and sometimes, what we find on the other side can be very disconcerting and in some cases overwhelming. But, that image of the empath who is constantly in the fetal position crying their eyes out is completely inaccurate. While empaths *can* get very emotional, only a small percentage of empaths are in that state permanently. After a while, empaths learn to cope with their gift. They tend to be aware of when they need to withdraw to prevent themselves from getting to that state.

8. Empaths are victims of trauma

Many victims of trauma can turn out to be empaths, but it's never caused by the trauma itself. Sometimes empaths can live perfectly lucky and stable lives, without much exposure to trauma at all, and they'll still strongly empathize with those who are different from them. This is what makes empaths so incredible. Most people need to experience something to learn from it, but empaths can absorb it instantly.

Chapter Two - Understanding the Empath Gift

Given everything that you've felt in your lifetime, you may feel reluctant to regard empathic qualities or abilities as a gift. And who can blame you? Your emotional journey up to this point has been akin to a rollercoaster ride. Most people have difficulty processing the emotions that they encounter. An empath can go through a whole menu of emotions before the morning is over and that is not all. You experience these emotions at a level of intensity that would normally erode what I like to call your emotion nerve points (they are like the numbers on the scale except, in this case, they are not assessing your weight but your limits). Many people would be broken if they were to experience a fraction of what you feel. At this point, you and your emotions are like a mountain with an active volcano. Your exterior hides the turmoil going on inside.

You are probably thinking, "This part-time writer and full-time empath is doing a poor job of selling the idea of seeing your empathic abilities as a gift." Well, that's because everything I've outlined can indeed be considered a weakness, if looked at through the wrong lens. But do you want to know a secret? You can easily make this weakness your superpower. You just need to know how.

Your ability to process a variety of emotions faster than the average person takes a lot of strength. The way you experience emotions and interactions with so much depth is a new kind of intelligence. And to be the human equivalent of a volcano? Come on! How awesome is that?

Many people consider the empath gift as a superpower, but it can actually be explained with science. Let's get deeper, shall we?

The Science Behind Empathy and Empaths

The explanations I've given for empathy, until now, have come from a psychological and experiential point of view. But what does science have to say about it? A surprising amount of research has been done on the subject, and there are more than a handful of theories out there to explain the empath experience. Some of these theories are hogwash and would not hold their own in any science court. I found a few quite interesting.

I examined as many scientific theories as possible in the course of my research. I sorted them into different folders: the utterly crazy, the science-fiction and the ones that truly gave me pause. I'll share the best theories that made the most sense to me. And how about just one of the silly ones to end on a laugh?

Theory #1:

The guys who spend their careers studying the brain had to get a top spot on this list and they did not disappoint. According to them, empaths behave the way they do because of the mirror effect. The mirror effect essentially tells us that when we see someone do something, the part of our brains that is responsible for executing those same actions is triggered. Without our realization, that action is executed neurologically. And even though in reality, that action was never carried out by us, our brain relays the information to us as though we've truly performed those actions. Subsequently, we experience the consequences of those actions first-hand as if they happened to us.

Let's say your friend tells you about their horrible breakup and how she had to pack up all her ex-partner's things into a suitcase. An empathic person immediately puts themselves in that position. It's almost as if you were there yourself, packing away the belongings of the person you're about to say goodbye to forever. You weren't there, but it feels real to you. You feel the sadness in its entirety. The part of your brain that would be active during that scenario is, indeed, active now. And all you needed was to hear the story from your friend. That's the life of an empath.

I am willing to bet that you've experienced this before. According to neuroscientists, when we see a person take a certain action, our brain tells us we've done the same thing and we experience what they feel. Neurologically speaking, we have actually walked a mile in their shoes.

The focus of the study was on empathy and not empaths in particular. And what it proved is that empathy is a choice. Yes, you read that right. The brain's transmission of signals may have sounded like an involuntary reaction such as a blinking reflex, but actually, the brain decides in less than a nanosecond whether it's going to engage in the mirror effect. The display of empathy becomes a choice. Psychopaths adamantly refuse to participate in that process by deliberately detaching themselves emotionally.

This second study fine-tuned the purpose of their research. It was not just about empathy in this case now. It was meant to explain why some people are more empathetic than others. The person in charge of this project decided against using the word 'empath.' Instead, 'altruist' was used. It is important to note that there are different types of altruists. You have the kin-based altruist. As the name implies, these guys are very empathetic towards people they consider closely related to them. A mother who keenly experiences the anguish of her child displays empathy like no other but that does not really make her an empath now, does it? The second group of altruists is classified under the reciprocity-based group. They are what I like to call, the scratch my back and I scratch your back type of giver. For them, a favor is a bond that they hold in high esteem with every intention of paying it forward no matter the cost to them. You ever watch those movies where the hero calls on an 'old friend' who owes him a favor to help him or her complete a mission. More often than not, this old friend dies but not before telling the hero that they have paid their debt [so sad when that happens]. Well, that is what we are talking about here. And then you have the third group of guys who do what they do simply because they genuinely care about the welfare of the person that they are doing this good deed for. They do not have to have a prior relationship with the person and as a matter of fact, the people in this group prefer to do their generous giving anonymously. These non-cape wearing heroes are classified as care-based altruists in the experiment and they were the main focus in this research. That said, let us get back to the research.

The participants in this where people who had done selfless acts like donating an organ to a complete stranger and other really cool stuff [that might have you considering what your next 'giving' would be if you know what I mean]. They were paired with people who have never done that and both groups were asked to look at different images showing different emotional expressions. Their brains were mapped to monitor their reaction to these images and the results documented. What it showed was that the amygdalae which are the portion of the brain responsible for processing emotions among other things appeared to be 8 percent bigger than the regular non-altruist in the group which is incredible. Of course, they also examined the other guys at the other end [the psychopaths] and what they found was that the amygdalae of psychopaths were 18 percent smaller than average. Now, this made sense to me. The idea that empaths are essentially people with a neurological bonus in the right are. Who knew 8 percent could make that much of a difference, right? But this brain phenomenon was not the only thing that stood them apart. Other aspects of their lives were studied and it showed that they [the care-based altruists] were evidently more humble than their peers. This is why they reacted to the pain and fears of complete strangers as though it were their own. And this brings us to the point of this research. The research was guided by the role that fear plays in the decisions made by altruists. Let me break that down for you.

Empath Survival Guide

Empaths are more than just givers. The key thing for empaths is experiencing the emotions of others as though it were their own. There are no limits to the range of emotions that they feel. They can feel the rage of others, the pain, and even their joys. This experiment focused on the giving aspect of empathy and not just the experiential element which is crucial to the full definition of an empath. The researchers wanted to find out if there was a way to clearly identify true empaths. I would say that what this was able to successfully achieve was tell us that some people are visibly more sensitive to the distress of others and are more motivated to act on it because they have processed and personalized the experience of the person in distress [again, the mirror effect comes to play here] but it still doesn't fully address the issue. However, I am willing to take that 8 percent bigger amygdalae they discovered.

This final research took theory from the lab into what I can best describe as 'hooey' waters. But it does make sense. Especially since it is coming from a professor of psychology. The first research I discussed here focused on the mirror effect. This research focused on what they called the mirror-touch synesthesia. According to the article I read, this is a phenomenon where the line between what is actually experienced and what is witnessed is blurred. In other words, what you see and what you feel are almost the same thing. Now mirroring the pain of another person is a fairly common experience. As a guy, you see a guy getting punched in his nether region can inspire a knee jerk reaction from you. Even girls can have the same reaction. However, the lines begin to blur when you don't just physically react to the pain of this person but you experience a corresponding pain in your nether region as well. The guys who conducted this research say that it is so rare that only about 2 percent of the population experience this.

This got me really interested because I have had a personal experience that I would say fit into this phenomenon. This was this period that I went to visit one of my very close cousins. I spent a few days at their home and the wife was very pregnant at the time. It was not one of those celebrity type pregnancies with the glowing skin and all-round gorgeousness. She had morning sickness, back pain, and acne on her face and body. I felt so sorry for her that at the end of my first day, I was puking a lot. At first, we thought that I had come down with the flu or something. I was quarantined in my room but at the end of day two, it was clear that I was mirroring her symptoms as I suddenly had acne on my face and chest. This was an isolated incident and I never gave it much thought after that period. But reading up on this research brought that to mind. Anyway, back to the research.

The gist of it was that they handed out materials to random people to assess their empathy levels and then a short test was conducted on them. The test was pretty straight-forward. The subject was to sit down and then a finger would tap one side of their face while they watched another person being tapped on their face also except it is on the opposite side. Then they were asked where they felt the tap. The general theory is that people who have the mirror-touch synesthesia were hesitant in responding because they were unsure where they felt the tap. Now the results were not entirely conclusive in supporting the existence of empaths. However, they showed us an aspect of empathy that may explain why certain people are highly 'empathic' than others. The inability to distinguish between one's own personal experience from that of others is a disturbing concept and clearly needs to be studied further but it does highlight the traits. My major takeaway from the results of that research is that there is an element of choice in the process. There isn't a brain design flaw that makes you more or less prone to being empathetic. And I think that all three types of research in a way support this. A part of you will react to certain situations a little differently than other people would but at the end of the day, this is not something you are doing without the participation of your will. In other words, empaths are not born empaths. It is a process. A combination of your upbringing, personal values and sometimes, a touch of biology.

That said, I did promise to look at one of the not so conventional scientific explanation behind the existence of empaths. I read a lot of articles on the subject and this particular one stood out for me. According to them, [I am not even going to waste your time by sending you over there with a link to read it] empaths are people who suffer from sensory processing disorder. If you spilled your coffee as you read that, you would be forgiven. But brace yourself, there is more. You see, they believe that empaths are people who are unable to accurately sort through the experiences that they get from the world around them because they are so sensitive to everything from sights to sounds and even smells. To paraphrase, "when life gets too overstimulating...some people even report dizziness, as well as increased anxiety". I had a very hard time relating to this as I am sure you would too. But after reading their description of empathic behaviors, it made sense that this would make sense to them. According to them [paraphrasing again], "enhanced empathy is the emotional equivalent of feeling pain at the gentlest touch on your arm". I would file this under 7234 things that an empath is not.

In conclusion, according to science, being an empath does not make you an oddball. You may react to things differently but that is just a part of what makes you special.

The Difference Between Cognitive, Emotional and Compassionate Empathy

When I started this journey a few years back to try and get a clear definition of what being is and what it should mean to me, I was fortunate to meet some amazing people in the process. One of them was and remains to this day a very good friend of mine. I meant Austin back in my college years right after I had come to a conclusion about science being unable to dispute the existence of empaths, the next step was to figure out how to get a handle on the whole thing and by that, I mean understanding us better. This friend of mine said one of the most profound things about being an empath. He said being an empath is like having a neural link to everyone you meet, see, hear or know about. Of course, it was a very nerdy thing to say but it was profound nonetheless. Empaths are connected to people by their emotional experiences. If this is the case, are all empaths cut from the same cloth? I mean, what happens to the empath with all these connections? How do they react? Do they experience things the same way? These questions got us thinking, if there is nothing scientifically that can differentiate one empath from another, there has to be a way to get to understand what makes empaths in general tick. And we started exploring the behavior of empaths.

Empaths react to emotions but how they react is what makes them unique. In my research, there are several types of empathy but I am going to focus on three different types (we will look at a few others later). And from these differentiations, I believe we are able to find the answers to why we act the way that we do. I will explore and explain each type one after the other and then we would bring it back to how all of that correlates with what we know about empaths.

Cognitive Empaths

These are empaths whose empathic abilities are tied to perspective. For them, the empathic experience has more to do with the fact that they are able to see things from the view of the person that they are empathizing with. Of all the three types of empathy I have come across, I think that cognitive empathy is the most detached form of empathy (well as detached as an empath can be) and it is also the most passive form of empathy. Empaths who fall in this category would make excellent mediators or diplomats as they have a propensity to see the view from both sides of the fence.

People who don't understand cognitive empaths think that they are logical emotionless beings who stick to the facts and ignore everything else but the opposite is the case. When these guys tell you that they understand how you feel, you better believe them because they actually do. Beyond emotions, a cognitive empath makes genuine effort to really "get" where you are coming from by deliberately taking a mental work in your shoes. And when they are in those shoes, they immerse themselves in the situation so that they can feel everything that you are feeling. I think that their response to people's emotional distress is less reactive and more pragmatic. And not pragmatic in the general sense of the word. Their practical approach to a solution would stem from their clear vision of where you are coming from.

For example, when a cognitive empath is proffering a solution to say a homeless person, it is going to go beyond a can of soup. And this is because they see the problem as a whole and not just the momentary discomforts that the person is currently experience. A typical cognitive empath would put themselves in the entire journey of a homeless person. They would look at the migration pattern of the homeless person, look at the weather conditions of the areas they are most likely going to spend the night, the hassle of moving around from place to place but without the luxury of having assorted clothes to match the seasons. So, you would find them doing something like buying or even designing a flexible outfit that can adapt to different weather conditions without requiring much maintenance. Not many people would this decision but after reading up on them, it made sense that the solution would be so practical but born from a place of understanding.

Emotional Empathy

This type of empathy is pretty much self-explanatory but to ensure that we are all on the same page, I am going to get into it anyway. Emotional empathy is an instinctive form of empathy where the empath reacts to the emotions of other people. Psychological profilers refer to this type of empathy as the most primitive form of empathy. If you go over what we discussed in the section that focused on the scientific theories behind empathy, that mirror effect that was highlighted in one of the studies is very applicable here.

An emotional empath may mirror the emotion that they see or hear in other people. But their emotional reaction does not always come from a place of logical understanding. It is just a reflex. However, just because it does not appear to be a thought-out process does not mean that emotional empaths are clueless about their reactions. As a matter of, the emotional quotient of emotional empaths is unusually high. They would be having a conversation with you and based their interpretation of certain body languages and the vibes (for lack of a better word) that you give off, they can pick on what you are feeling and mirror either the same emotion or a corresponding emotion that would make you feel better. The general scope is that these guys are very emotionally intelligent.

One very common misconception people have about emotional empaths is that they are very emotional and would probably cry or lose control of their emotions at the drop of the hat. The reality is different. Their emotional intelligence affords them the ability to also sense their own emotions and then put a stopper on it before it gets out of hand. They can accurately detect emotions, reflect those emotions and sometimes even deflect those emotions before the person experiencing them even realizes what is going on. They have this innate gift of being able to make the people around feel better.

Compassionate Empathy

Now, this right here is the most active form of empathy. It combines aspects of both the cognitive empathy and the emotional empathy in that the compassionate empath is able to see things from the other person's point of view and then react based on the understanding that they now have. The emotional empath is the guy that we all know and have stereotyped as the typical empath while the compassionate empath is the one who we are all trying to become. The qualities of the compassionate empath almost put them on that celestial level because they sound almost too good to be true but that is who they are essentially.

An compassionate empath is the kind of person who would know that her best friend's heartbreak playlist is a sign that all in not well in the romance department and more than just acknowledging that this is what is going on, they would take it a step further by organizing just the right kind of event or activity that would get the said friend out of their funk and into a new groove. We all want a compassionate empath in our corner because they make life that much easier to navigate.

Now looking back on these three empaths, you would see that they each have their advantages and disadvantages (some more than the other) but they all serve a purpose. The end goal for empaths is to become the compassionate empath because they seem to have a healthy balance of action and reactions. One thing I observed across the board is that you can work towards improving aspects of yourself if you feel that you lean too much in one category. For instance, if you find that you are too pragmatic in your dealings with people, you may want to train yourself to be more emotionally intelligent. Don't get me wrong. I don't think that being practical is wrong. But sometimes, you can get a little too disconnected from the present reality because you are so focused on the bigger picture. A little emotional intelligence would go a long way in fixing this. As for the emotional empath, sometimes, the people around you are going to need more than a show of feelings to get them through situations. Getting to understand what they are really going through rather than relying on your instincts alone can help you be more 'useful' in times of crisis.

What makes an empath?

At the end of the first segment in this chapter, there was one big lesson we learned about what empaths are not… they are not created even though in some cases, they are born the way they are (very confusing, I know= but we will get to that in a bit). Granted, there are some biological markers that would play a role in how you process certain things, however, it does not ultimately define you. One of the biological factors attributed to certain empathic behaviors is the amygdalae. The science guys tell us that empaths have their amygdalae a little bit bigger than those of their average counterpart but there has also been some talk about people with larger amygdalae having deep seethed anxiety issues. According to that research, certain events (related to fear and anxiety) can trigger a growth of new cells in this area of the brain which in turn increases the size of this part of the brain leading to more anxiety. Seeing as empaths are not exactly riddled with anxiety, you can't blame biology for this one.

Some people try to trace their empathic abilities to a particular event, trauma or memory in their lives despite the fact that they are unable to remember a time when they were never the way they are now. Admitting to abilities being caused or triggered by some kind of tragedy would imply that the abilities were dormant and somehow, they were woken. Not only does this sound unrealistic, but it also sounds like something that was ripped off the plot of a low-budget sci-fi movie… cryptic, bizarre and false. If nothing else, the opposite happens. A tragic event can trigger a shut down of your empathic abilities. In subsequent chapters, we will discuss this in detail but take it from me, empathy is not born out of one's personal experience. I should point out here that there are certain experiences you would have that would cause you to empathize with anyone who goes through something similar. However, as I am sure we have learned so far, the display of empathy is not what automatically makes you an empath. There is more to it than that.

Until scientific research proves otherwise, rather than looking for one element as the spark that set off the who empathic nature in motion, think of your existence as the result of many factors coming together to create one awesome you. There is a biological component there to kick things off, a smidgen of experiences to open you up to more emotions, a little bit of social conditioning and a healthy dose of willpower.

5 other types of empaths you didn't know about

When we got into this segment about the different types of empaths, I did say we would look at other types of empaths. If you were unable to identify with the other forms of empathy, there is a great chance that you just might find your fit here. Mind you, these types of empaths are not very common but they have very unique identifiable traits and I will go over those traits briefly.

Geomantic Empath: The emotions of a geomantic empath is attuned to the environment that they are in. Their empathic abilities feed off the energies of whatever location they find themselves in. A typical geomantic empath would tell you that certain places make them feel a specific kind of emotion. They are usually drawn to places that either has a rich history or places that are considered sacred like temples, churches and so on.

Plant Empath: These guys have what we all call a green thumb and this is because plants always seem to thrive better under their care. But that has more to do with their natural intuition for the needs of the plants than their knowledge about planting itself. Plant empaths tend to thrive in jobs or businesses that revolve around the plant industry.

Animal Empath: Like the plant empaths, animal empaths are attuned to the needs of animals. They can somehow sense what animals need. The common term for them is animal whisperers. However, unlike plant empaths who connects with almost all kinds of plants, animal empaths are likely attuned to a specific animal. So, it is not out of the ordinary to find animal empaths whose empathy is towards cats, dogs or even birds.

Intuitive Empath: Also called claircognizant empaths, these guys can intuitively pick up on the emotions of other people without being told about them. They are the kind of empaths who are not easily swayed by the emotional expressions of people because they can sense the true nature of the person's emotions hidden underneath the façade that they present no matter how well constructed it is.

Physical/Medical Empath: A medical empath can almost immediately sense when a person's body is out of order for health reasons. They pick up on the energy coming off people that they meet and they can read that energy the same way a meteorologist would read the weather.

Chapter Three - The Empath Reality

After looking at empathy and the empath from both a mythical and scientific point, it is time to get real with what this is all about. And by real, I mean getting to the nitty-gritty details of the everyday life of an empath. Beyond the digital hype that has been amplified by the media's portrayal of empaths, there is the reality and it is not always pleasant. This reality is the reason you probably picked up this book in the first place. The 'gift' of seeing the world through the multi-colored lenses of emotions comes at a price. And the sooner you understand the price you are paying, the easier it would be to stop the spiral down the proverbial rabbit hole. As you read further, you may have to confront some startling truths. It may get a little uncomfortable but I promise you that it gets better in the end. Instead of looking at this as a forecast of doom, think of it as your private coming out party where you get to see yourself reflected in the pages of this book in all of your shining glory... flaws, strengths and all.

The Dark Side of Being an Empath

We know that empaths are generally emotionally intuitive on some level even if what they are attuned to might be different. However, this experience leaves them emotionally raw and sensitive most of the time. But emotional sensitivity is not the only thing that they have to deal with. Reflecting on my life as well as the information I was able to put together during my research, I made a list of a few of the things that almost all empaths would struggle with.

1. Empaths have a tendency to become depressed: For empaths, it is a constant battle to sort through the myriad of emotions that they feel. First, they have to work hard at keeping their emotions in check. As I have established, most empaths are emotionally intelligent and as a result, you won't find them losing control of their emotions but what most people do not realize is how difficult it is to do this. After putting a lid on their emotions, the next thing they have to do is determine if the emotions that they are struggling with is their own in the first place. Given their ability to absorb the emotions of other people, it is understandable that those feelings can eventually become mixed up with their own personal opinions and emotions. These frequent internal battles can lead to depression.

2. Empaths are typically emotionally exhausted: Dealing with emotions at the frequency and intensity that empaths do is very draining. This leads to an emotional fatigue

3. Empaths treat themselves as second class citizens: I am not sure if this is tied to the depression or the fact that they are always at the brink of exhaustion. But most empaths operate their personal lives on reserve because of all the other stuff that they have to deal with. Their impulsive need to help other people make it difficult for them to prioritize themselves.

4. Empaths struggle with guilt: Helping people is primal instinct for empaths. When they are confronted by any emotional puzzle, they have an almost compulsive need to put the pieces together and, in a situation where they fail to do so, they take this as a personal loss. They feel that they have failed the person or persons involved and this guilt could eat at them for a very long time. Sometimes, they task themselves with making up for this perceived failure by bending over backward to please and appease the "wronged" person.

5. Empaths are emotional sponges: Soaking up the energy of a room might sound cool until you find yourself soaking up more negative energy than a person should have to deal with. And while empaths have the ability to turn off the emotional faucet just as fast as they turn it on, their guilt-ridden nature makes them more inclined to deal with the negative stuff that people put out for longer than the average human. Coping with negative people is one thing but taking on some aspects of that negativity, that is a different ball game entirely and not a fun one at that. This brings us to the next big issue.

6. Empaths have a tendency to be in toxic relationships: Every one of the traits that we have looked at so far bring s us to this point. Because of the giving nature of the empath, they tend to attract the kind of people who would deliberately take advantage of that. And even when an empath is in a relationship where they are being taken advantage of, you would be hard-pressed to find them getting out of that situation willingly. Some of those who have successfully left those relationships end up guilt-tripping themselves back into those toxic situations.

These dark traits attributed to empaths does not essentially mean that all empaths have to be this way. In other words, you don't have to live with the darkness. However, there are certain behavioral patterns that have to be dealt with in order to deal with the darkness. Being an empath may make you prone to certain things like the depression we talked about but there are habits that you have that could drive your life to the point where everything that you do is characterized by depression. In this next segment, we are going to be looking at some of those habits.

5 Bad Habits that Empaths Must Let Go

1. Saying yes to everything: Empaths are natural people pleasers. This makes them more inclined to say yes even when that yes does not benefit them in any way. In the workplace, this can leave the empath stuck in a career rut as they find themselves spending more hours completing other people's project instead of focusing on growing their careers.

2. The need to fix everything: The phrase, "if it is not broke, don't fix it' tends to fly over the head of an empath. A bird with broken wings needs to be nursed back to health, a child with a sad history needs a

little light to let go of that dark past but a grown person with deep anger management issues need to make the choice to be better and no amount of loving or caring can get them to that place without their own consent. Empaths need to know when to leave things well alone.

3. Not speaking up for themselves: Empaths are no pushovers. At least not in the basic sense of it. However, they like to leave the floor open to other people to air their views and feelings while their own feelings are out in the back burner. This is born out of goodwill as they feel that the other person venting would help them release whatever they are feeling but it becomes a burden if you as an empath frequently have to hold back on saying how you really feel. This leads to a lot of repressed emotions which we know is a mental ticking time bomb.

4. Choosing to spend more time in their head: It is okay to step back every other day and take a few moments to be with yourself. But when it becomes a regular habit, it can be detrimental to you. It actually makes sense that you want to avoid dealing with all those emotions which come as part of the package when you have to deal with people. However, if you let go of most of the habits listed here, you would find it a lot easier to deal with people.

5. Taking things too personally: When you are sensitive and are an emotional sponge, everything that happens around you may begin to feel like it is all about you. Certain harmless comments or actions may be interpreted as a vendetta directed at you. I would say that has a lot to do with your need to piece together emotional puzzles, therefore, everything would seem connected to something which is then translated into personal meaning. But the truth is, things happen simply because they just happen.

The 5 Common Health Problems of Empaths

For the most part, due to the highly emotional nature of an empath, their health struggles are more psychological and mental than they are physical. So, a lot of things you would see in this segment have more to do with the mental illnesses than anything else. However, the lifestyle of the empath could influence the health issues they face more than their nature as empaths. Still, we cannot ignore the role that their nature plays in the process.

1. Anxiety: Most empaths battle with anxiety. The level of anxiety that they suffer varies from mild to severe and emotional empaths tend to have the most severe cases of anxiety when compared to others. Physical empaths are another group of empaths whose anxiety levels soar through the roof especially if they have to deal with crowds but it often veers into another mental health territory like panic disorders and we will get to that in a bit. Their ability to overcome or at least manage their anxiety is largely dependent on their self-awareness about who they are.

2. Depression: Given their propensity to juggle emotions at the same time, it is not surprising that they also have to deal with issues of depression from time to time. When they are not picking up on other people's emotions, they have to deal with guilt, isolation and their own personal drama. It is almost as if they can't catch a break. In addition to being self-aware, empaths need to talk with fellow empaths or therapist to help them sort through their emotions.

3. High Blood Pressure: High blood pressure is strongly linked to lifestyle and diet. However, stress and anxiety (which we know empaths are prone to) have been known to cause temporary spikes in blood pressure. The effect of anxiety on blood pressure does not last long but if it happens regularly, this blood pressure spikes can go ahead to cause damage to major organs in the body. Empaths should learn relaxation techniques that would help them bring their blood pressure down when they have an anxiety attack. Also, they need to watch out for the kind of habits they pick up to cope with anxiety. Habits like smoking can go on to complicate their health.

4. Panic Disorders: This usually happens when a person's stress and anxiety levels experienced are soaring really high. This is brought on by stressful situations and for empaths, this typically means when they are surrounded by a lot of people with all of these emotions hitting them from different directions. Panic disorders are not necessarily life-threatening but the experience is horrible. Seeking the help of a medical professional goes a long way in the treatment and management of panic disorders.

5, Agoraphobia: Everyone has some form of phobia but there are phobias that are peculiar to people with certain traits. Agoraphobia is a form of anxiety that causes a person to be afraid of being in crowded spaces or places where they get a sense that they cannot escape. Agoraphobia is best treated in its early stages. The more it is left unattended, the more overpowering it comes. It is not life-threatening in the physical sense but it can rob you of living a fulfilled life. The experience is so much worse for an empath.

As you have read, the health issues of an empath are somewhat interrelated. Again, your lifestyle does play an important role in how healthy you are. But having a very good understanding of your personality as an empath and being very self-aware as to how things really work for you would go a long way to helping you establish a good foundation for a healthy life. As you have seen, prevention is way better than treatment for most of the ailments here. The general assumption is that it is specific situations that trigger these ailments and while that is true, that is not the only trigger out there. There are people who are classified as 'toxic' especially for an empath. These people are not necessarily evil but their behavior, mannerisms and personality traits make the life of an empath more complicated than it should be. So, in keeping with the theme of prevention, let us look at a few personalities you should definitely avoid as an empath.

The Personalities that Empaths Can't be Around

Narcissists:

These personality types are so into themselves that they would fail to see the harm their neglect and selfishness is causing the empath in their lives. Their actions may not be out of malice but the sensitive empath should not have to deal with this daily. It becomes even worse when the person is an abusive narcissist.

Manipulators:

This is another breed of selfish personalities who are willing to go the extra mile to make the people around them do the things that they want to do even if those things benefit no one else but themselves. Manipulators would play on the guilt that empaths feel to get them to do their bidding. This creates a very toxic cycle for the empath.

Abusers:

Nobody should be around abusers but this is especially true for empaths. Most abusers combine the traits of a narcissist and a manipulator in addition to their personal insecurities and constant need for control. An empath is actually the one person who can connect well enough with an abuser to even see things from their perspective and in a sad way, understand where they are coming from well enough to dare, I say it, justify the abuse that they are suffering. No one should have to go through that.

Chapter Four - The Injured Empath

In the first chapter, I shared some of the biggest misconceptions that people have about empaths. One of them was the idea that empaths are broken people; that for them to be able to connect to the feelings and experiences that a lot of people have, they must have walked the same path. By now, you know that this isn't the case. An empath does not need to have a first-hand experience to truly understand what you feel. However, through their abilities, they can get front row seats to your pain and know exactly how it feels. That said, it does not mean that there are no broken empaths. Being broken is part of the human experience and as long as you are human, you are bound to have a phase where you are broken. The loss of something of value whether an object, a person or even ideas that we have can cause a pain so intense that you feel crushed by the weight of it. This is the point where a person gets broken.

There is absolutely nothing wrong in being broken. The problem comes when you let that experience characterize everything that you do going forward. You have to understand that it is a human nature to fall, but it is also our nature to rise. Now rising does not necessarily mean that everything would right back to status quo. When you fall down and get injured, it hurts. Physiologically, a few cells die in the area where the injury occurred. But as the body begins the healing process, a few new cells are born. As the healing progresses, the pain begins to recede until all that is left to remind you of the injury is the scar. In the same manner, when life kicks us down, we get hurt and broken. But if you let it, the brokenness heals as begin to rise. However, we are left with the scars of those experiences. If the memories from those experiences are not brought into focus and the emotions that were stirred at that point in time not addressed, the emotional scars that will develop can affect the quality of life as well as the opportunities that you have later on.

An injured person is one carries the emotional scars from their past wherever they go. For an injured empath, the experience is even worse they are relieving these emotions at intensity levels that are so high that the past would seem like it only just happened yesterday. Each moment brings them a visit from the past and cages them in the present so that they are oblivious to the joys that are going on and unable to move forward to the future that they deserve. Injured empaths are curiously like the Mimosa Pudica also known as the touch me not plant. The second you touch them; their leaves close up. Incidentally, another nickname for the touch me not plant is 'the sensitive plant'. Their reaction to touch is the same way that an injured empath would react to life. Their emotional scars are so deep and the effect is so intense that every time life singles them out for a new experience whether good or bad, they quickly recoil to the 'safe' haven that they have created for themselves. The sad part is that this so-called safe haven is anything but safe. It is like a room with a living breathing nuclear reactor in it that draws its energy from the darkness surrounding it.

Another sad fact is that like the average person, most empaths won't even realize what is happening to themselves until either they are consumed by their past (an emotional nuclear explosion) or something disrupts the cycle of behavior that led down that destructive path, to begin with. It doesn't help that the coping mechanisms for most empaths are self-destructive behaviors, to begin with. For starters, there is that reclusive behavior. There is nothing wrong in being a recluse, but you take things to the extreme when paranoia sets in and you begin to hide even from your own shadow. The only way forward is to allow our minds to heal and recover from the emotional injuries sustained. When a physical wound is being treated, the very first thing any doctor would do is to make an attempt to treat the life-threatening symptoms of the wound. For emotional injuries, I would say the equivalent of that is coming out of your shell. Even if you are going to stay inside of your house cooped up, the least you can do is to pick up the phone and call somebody and then just talk. It does not have to be about what you are going through. The fact that you are having a conversation alone is going to be like coming up for a breath of fresh air after in an oxygen-deprived space.

The next step is to go the source of the wound which in the case of an empath is not always the incident that you think triggered the pain in the first place. It is usually something called compassion fatigue. And that is what the rest of this chapter is going to be about.

What is Compassion Fatigue?

In very lay terms, compassion fatigue happens when a person becomes emotionally desensitized to the needs, pains and sufferings of other people. Compassion fatigue is also known as secondary traumatic stress and has been associated with people who have been constantly exposed stories and experiences of tragedies for so long that it would appear as though their nerve endings just snapped and stopped functioning. Now, you may be inclined to think that this means the person experiencing the compassion fatigue (in this case an empath) would move from their end of the scale and tip towards the section where you have the psychopaths. This is not so. People who suffer from compassion fatigue don't suddenly become dead to their emotions. In fact, they become even more acutely aware of it. what happens is that they internalize these emotions that they feel and are unable or unmotivated to act on it.

Let me give you a brief rundown of my theory on the subject. When you are confronted with a situation where a person that you know on some level is going through a very tragic experience, you are instinctively inclined to want to help. You find a way to provide a solution for that person. Even if you cannot completely avert the tragedy, you want to do all that you can to improve the situation. When you achieve this, there is a reward section of your brain that is triggered. You feel very good about this good deed that you are done. In that moment, the sun shines a little brighter, the world appears to have a little more color and life, in general, is very fantastic. This perhaps explains people have been trying to convince us that doing good does some with its own special kind of reward. This is all good and well. After living through this wonderful experience which essentially is a psychological feedback from your good deed, you are inclined to repeat this process again. It doesn't matter if the circumstances are the same or different, you want to help this new person. For empaths, this experience can be very addictive. They want to keep doing these good deeds and continue reliving the psychological aftermath. It is like a high except that there is no drug that can quite match the effect. But when happens when the good deed that you carried out is unable to make a difference?

This is where the story takes a slightly darker turn. Let us take this same scenario we mentioned earlier but with a not so positive outcome. You are confronted with a situation where someone you know on some level is going through some kind of tragic experience. As a good friend, colleague or whatever your relationship is with that person, you step in to help because that is just what you do. Now you offer this help in the hope that the tragedy can be averted or in the very least, the circumstance can be improved but instead, nothing happens. Or even worse, things become even more tragic than you met them. You are now forced to watch this person live through the pain and trauma from their experience until it either ends their life or ends your relationship with them. As an empath, you would get some feedback from their pain and this registers on your psyche. It doesn't stop you from trying to help people but there is a part of you that struggles with the following;

1. Your failure to help this person

2. Your second-hand experience of their pain
3. Your anxiety losing another friend or relationship in the same way

Things get a little more complicated for empaths who work in specific professions where they are constantly faced with tragedy. For empaths who have to deal with this occasionally with their circle of friends, the progression of compassion fatigue is slower. But for people whose occupations are in the health sector like nurses, care-givers, psychology and so on, there is a high risk of developing compassion fatigue within a shorter timeframe. People who work as lawyers as also susceptible to it. Empaths in these fields sometimes end up being unable to differentiate their work life from their personal lives to you would find the emotional burn out affection their ability to connect emotionally with other people too.

Having all of this in mind, you cautiously approach other relationships. Now, we all know that at some point, life happens. This other relationship may not have the same tragic elements as the previous but even the slightest hint at tragedy might get your instincts kicking in on overdrive. Obviously, you rush in to help. This time around, you are just as anxious about the results of your efforts as you are about the person's wellbeing that even if your effort is rewarded by an aversion of tragedy, your only psychological reward would be relief that all works out. The rush is not the same this success would seem to highlight your failure. And this drives you into a cycle where you keep trying to make up for the proverbial one that got away. If your effort to help fails like the first time around, you are flung deeper into that cycle and anxiety takes deeper roots in your psyche. The more fixes and saves you do, the more you want to do, but this is no longer inspired by the high which we talked about initially. It is now about balancing the scales. The stress and anxiety that comes with each case that you face pushes you closer to the line where it is no longer about helping people but simply getting through the day. At this point, you are having secondary traumatic stress.

Signs of an Injured Empath

The point where an empath experiences compassion fatigue is where the emotional injury we discussed earlier is rooted. As I said, it is not isolated to an event or a singular experience so you cannot take a mental trip to this specific spot, snap your fingers and find closure. It is a little more complicated than that. Thankfully, you can determine if you have arrived at this point even though you don't know what led you here. If you recall, I painted a picture of a safe haven likened to a room housing an active nuclear reactor and how toxic that environment can be for you. In this section, we are going to highlight all these factors that make being in the state where you are dangerous and then we will talk about how to cross those hurdles.

1. A Keen Sense of Hopelessness that Results in Detachment

If you find yourself unable to summon a genuine feeling of optimism for the things that you do, you may have subscribed to that feeling of hopelessness. When you have a situation that requires your help and you do it not because you are certain or in the very least hoping that it would make a difference, but because you are obligated to, you might be having compassion fatigue. In this case, the need to play out your role takes priority over the needs of the person. Everything about caring for this person becomes a routine activity for you. The biggest clue in this regard would be the fact that you are unable to look past today because you feel that there is a very strong possibility that there won't be a tomorrow.

2. Apathy Toward the People You Care for

This is a form of detachment but not necessarily an absence of care because as an empath on some level, you always care. But the experiences you have had has groomed you to the point that you have become indifferent to the entire experience. You are more matter-of-factly in the way you care and help. Since your indifference does not come from a place of malice or ill will, you will always show up. However, your indifference has been constructed as a wall to protect you from the tragedy you are already expecting so that 'when' it happens, you are not so visibly affected by it. If you find yourself thinking this way, know that you are probably experiencing compassion fatigue

3. Elevated Stress Levels

In the face of tragedy, we experience a lot of things emotionally. These emotions cause stress. Now there is the normal stress level of the average person and then you have abnormal stress levels. Compassion fatigue triggers a high level of stress even in situations that have very little similarities to the events that you can call the ground zero of your emotional trauma. In addition to all the other symptoms mentioned here, if you discover that you are reacting adversely to stress such as breathlessness, inability to focus, severe anxiety and panic attacks, you are having compassion fatigue

4. Nightmares and disruption in sleep routines

Nightmares and a change in sleep routine is typically a sign of an internal struggle with some kind of unresolved emotional trauma. When dealing with the pain of other people trigger nightmares and sleeplessness, it is possible that you are having an emotional burnout. Your mind is unable to cope with the situation and even worse, it is unable to cope with the fact that you cannot cope with the situation… a classic nightmare for empaths.

5. Struggling with feelings of Self-Contempt

Empaths already have a thing for guilt-tripping themselves. When they hit the compassion fatigue point, this guilt grows into self-contempt as they feel a sense of disappointment in their inadequacies. This is because empaths measure their sense of self-worth with their ability to provide help and 'fix' things. Failure to do this causes self-doubt which evolves into guilt and grows into contempt.

If you look at all of the symptoms listed, you would see the progression of the internal struggle brought on by compassion fatigue. An outward experience becomes an inward struggle that becomes all about them which can be pretty selfish and a strong contradiction to their normally selfless nature. The inward struggle is what keeps them in that 'room' we talked about earlier. They find it difficult to come of this mental space that they have created because they have adorned themselves with the persona of a victim. Somehow, this thing that totally was about them has now made them the victim. In the next chapter, we discuss this in detail.

Beware: The Victim Complex

Self-pity is a normal experience for everyone. We have moments when we fall into that woe-is-me hole but as long as you don't hold on to that hat for longer than necessary, you are going to be fine. Victim complex, on the other hand, is choosing to lay on a bed of misery, covering up yourself with your failures or the list of everything that has gone wrong and just lying there in it. For an empath, having a case of compassion fatigue can create a segue into a full-blown victim complex experience. The general experience of the victim complex would see the person experiencing it deferring all responsibility to everyone and everything but themselves. But in the case of the empath, they take the whole blame for everything and then somehow make the entire experience about them. I know that this seems a little confusing but let me explain it anyway.

An empaths victim complex is not about making themselves the star of the show by abdicating any blame or responsibility that was assigned to them. They don't wear the sad-is-me crown to make other people feel sorry for them. If anything, they would hate to be that person because there is a very strong possibility that they deal with such people on a regular basis. The victim complex for empaths come in when they internalize their failures, store up the pain that they have absorbed on the outside and then sort of idolize it on the inside. Most injured empaths have a victim complex. They do not have the resilience needed to cope with their personal failures. Now let me digress a little bit here. A personal failure for an empath goes beyond their inability to successfully complete a project. That kind of failure is one that they can deal with. But when they are unable to fix their people projects, that kind of failure seeps deep into their minds and they take it personally. They can get so fixated on it that they work twice as hard to 'redeem' themselves with other people projects.

Besides the increased risk of failure associated with taking on more people project, there is the problem of not dealing with the initial failure. As a result, any people project that is taken on would only echo the failure and the longer they deal with this, the more intense the situation would get. The intensity of the emotions experienced would lead to an emotional burn out that we have now identified as compassion fatigue which leads us to where we are now. A victim complex sounds like something harmless but here is the part I am pretty sure that you did not know. The victim complex is the element that keeps the wheels spinning in this self-destructive cycle. It is the bars that would keep you locked in that 'safe' room that stops you from living your life. I read of an ancient religious group where believers or practitioners were physically chastised whenever they err. These chastisements were so terrible that they would be in physical pain for months on end. The scars that they bore on their bodies told tales of horror and trauma so horrendous that you would think that they served in slaves camps or some kind of torture chamber. The reality was that all of these injuries were self-inflicted.

The need to make yourself pay for perceived failures by locking up yourself in this 'safe' haven is the emotional equivalent of the self-inflicted injuries on those believers. Take your freedom today by learning to prioritize your self-care just as much as you value the care of other people. Most importantly, you need to stop looking at people as projects that you need to fix. I have mentioned this before and later in the book, we would discuss this in-depth. But if you do anything today, let it be that you acknowledge your importance and treat yourself accordingly. That said, I would like us to look at another self-destructive behavior that could ruin the life of an empath

The Truth About Empaths and Addiction

The emotional turmoil, as well as the intrinsic nature of the empath, make them a perfect candidate for addiction. Their need to get out of their own heads every other day means they are open to trying out coping mechanisms that would offer them this. The fact that this emotional turmoil is an ongoing struggle means that they are more likely to keep going back to continue using this coping mechanism especially if it successfully provides the temporary fix that they need. When you try something for so long, it becomes a routine. Over time, a routine becomes a habit and with habits, especially bad habits, you get addicted. A coping mechanism could be anything from drug use to comfort eating to watching porn. And the thing with these things I have mentioned is that you never really see it as a problem until it is too late.

In my experience, food was my vice. It started out innocently enough. I would come back home from work, tired and exhausted. However, no matter how exhausted I was, sleep was something that eluded me. So, I would get out of bed, fix myself something sweet in the kitchen and then plop myself down on the couch and binge-watch those terrible television shows. In those moments, I was completely calm, very relaxed and certainly not thinking about the horrible day I had at work. After some time, I decided to upgrade my couch meal to something with a more 'luxurious' feel. I would stop by at the pastry shop on my way home and pick up an array of sweet treats and then repeat my routine in front of the TV. A few months later, the couch didn't feel comfortable enough so I got a larger screen and then took the show into my bedroom. For the better part of a year, I spent my nights eating junk food in bed while watching junk TV. As you can imagine, it started showing on my waistline. My old clothes stopped fitting me and then I started feeling more self-conscious about how I looked.

I had friends who were too polite to point out the physical changes but I could see the way they looked at me. Then I had 'friends' who had no problems telling me exactly how they felt. Their words made me feel even more horrible about myself and when I felt really bad, it meant I spent a lot more at the pastry shop. My lowest point which also turned out to be my turning point was this particular day when I was eating this really delicious donut on my way home (it had gotten to the point that I couldn't wait to get home anymore). The donut slipped from my hand and fell on the floor. It was probably around 7 pm and there weren't that many people on the street. I know because I glanced around and then I did the unthinkable. I bent down and pick my fallen donut off the sidewalk. I blew on it and ate it with I was still bent there with one knee on the floor. Just then, I caught my reflection in one of the storefronts and I did not like the person who was starring back at me. To make a long story short, I had a good cry when I got home and that was the beginning of my journey to this point where I am writing my story in a book. Today, I still have an addiction but I have made a conscious effort to ensure that my addiction is healthy. I have a habit for different moods. When I am angry, I paint. When I feel a little blue, I get on the treadmill or put on my boxing gloves and work up a good sweat. When I am anxious, I write.

You are going to have to find out what works for you but it starts with you admitting to yourself that this seemingly harmless habit you have engaged may not be entirely healthy for you. People think that drug is the only harmful addiction, I have read about empaths who are addicted to the misery they are facing that they would willingly self-sabotage any shot that they have at happiness. It is sad to witness but this is the reality. When you are experiencing those floods of emotions, what are the things that you do to cope? Do those things add value to you as they make you feel better or do they take away something valuable from you in exchange for making you feel better? Addiction for empaths is a serious problem and it needs to be taken seriously or else you would end up complicating things for yourself. Today, the goal is to get you out of that sense of false security that you have created for yourself. This book is a guide on how you can survive in the world as an empath. For that to happen, you need to step out of your enclave and into the real world because not only will you survive it, you will thrive in it.

Chapter Five - The Dangers of Being an Empath

In the previous chapter, we explored some of the dangers of being an empath. In this chapter we are going to delve into the dark side of things. Leading up to this point, empaths have been regarded as beings in possession of supernatural power. That is cool and I honestly wished it was that way 100% of the time but there's a price that empaths and it goes beyond the emotional struggles that we have. Because of the intricate nature of the empath, they tend to attract a certain kind of people to themselves. We have talked about the need for the empath to fix people. Whenever they encounter people with emotional struggles and some psychological pain, the first instinct is to want to help but we forget that not all the people that come to us want to be helped. Some people are programmed or to be more specific, they are emotionally programmed to take advantage of the help that we wish to offer and this is where the problem begins.

The empire's desire to help attract a specific kind of people and more often than not, these people fall into the category of those with a psychological need to take advantage of others. Sometimes these relationships start out with good intentions. But in time, their predatory nature quickly takes over and they end up destroying the empath from within. This is the danger that all empaths face. In the previous chapter, I talked about certain kinds of people that empaths should avoid and one of those people is the narcissist. The narcissist is a special breed of individuals and their qualities go beyond their love for themselves. They are recognized for their skills at masterfully manipulating people to do their bidding and the nature of the empath make them more prone to the manipulations of a narcissist.

Identifying a narcissist

From old literature, we are led to believe that a narcissist is someone who is vain; a person who is obsessed with their physical looks and how they present themselves to the world. In psychology, it's a lot deeper than that as narcissist take on a different form. One of their unappealing qualities is the fact that they have a great sense of self-importance but for someone who is not very observant, this attribute is not something that you would pick on right away. Their victim mentality provides a great mask for their true personality but more importantly, they have a way of blending in perfectly with the rest of the society which makes it somewhat difficult to identify them. Some narcissists are simply harmless in their relationships. Narcissists who fall in this category are people who are self-aware and have worked on the negative side of themselves. But then you have the narcissists on the other spectrum who are terrible as companions because their sense of self-importance is so grand that they are willing to compromise the feelings and emotions of other people just to satisfy their own needs. Narcissists are selfish, self-important and self-righteous but ironically, they are the list self-aware people.

Based on the description I have given, I am sure you can understand why narcissists are people that can be very difficult to deal with even for anyone who is not an empath. However, if you're able to understand them, you get a better sense of how to relate with them especially if you are an empath. According to psychology, there are different types of narcissists. You have the grandiose narcissist. These guys are basically people who have a huge ego. To deal with them, you need to offer up a lot of attention in the form of praise. This feeds their ego and makes them much more manageable in relationships. Then you have the vulnerable narcissists. You can identify them by the victim mentality that they seem to wear like a badge. Everything that happens in life seems to revolve around them. It could be raining somewhere in China and causing floods in certain villages but the vulnerable narcissist living a few continents away would find a way to make it about them. They have a very high tendency to complain about anything and everything. To manage a relationship with them, they need to be given attention in the form of emotional support. And then finally, you have the malignant narcissists. These guys are the ones you need to watch out for. The other two types of narcissist mentioned earlier can be emotionally exhausting to deal with but as far as damages go, as long as you can give them what they want in terms of their emotional needs, they are fine. Malignant narcissists, on the other hand, display a lack of empathy on the level that is so high that psychologists compare them with psychopaths.

To identify the malignant narcissist in your life you would need to be very attentive. As I said earlier, a narcissist has a way of blending in with everyone. So, there aren't really factors that make them stand out from the crowd. In fact, psychologists believe that narcissist are usually happier than most people who have been diagnosed with some form of psychological disorder. To keep things in perspective, I compiled a list that will help you identify a narcissist specifically, the malignant narcissist. This list is based on certain traits. Be guided though, you need a clinical psychologist to accurately diagnose a malignant narcissist but until that happens, here are few red flags that should make you wary of any person who displays more than one of these traits.

1. They have a strong sense of self-importance
2. They are very obsessed with their idea of what they consider as ideal (the ideal wife, the ideal friend, the ideal love, the ideal relationship)
3. They have a very strong sense of entitlement
4. They have an unrealistic expectation about things in general
5. They have a tendency to use other people to get what they want
6. They are very manipulative
7. They lack empathy and display an unwillingness to recognize the needs and emotions of other people

There is a general saying that opposites attract. Perhaps this is the foundation of the relationship between the narcissists and an empath, because, on a surface level, it is hard to determine why someone as sensitive and generous as an empath will fall for someone as cold and calculating as a narcissist but when you explore the dynamics of the relationship it does make sense why these 2 opposites would be attracted to each other. However, this relationship can only be described as a recipe for disaster. To better understand why this continues to happen, I felt it will be important to look at why these 2 people would choose each other and to determine that, we need to look at what each personality would stand to gain from this relationship.

Why Narcissists Are Drawn to Empaths

If you look at the traits of a narcissist, you would see that for them every relationship that they get into is a one-sided business transaction designed to favor just one party. I leave you with just one guess as to who that party is. A typical malignant narcissist is very calculating and they never enter into anything without a plan on how they can take. From the onset, they can instinctively recognize people who would give them a hard time achieving their goals. They hate people that they cannot manipulate and in the workplace, or environments where they are required to team up with other people, you would find the narcissist at loggerheads with these types of people. To look at what a narcissist would be drawn to, let us take a look at how relationships work with a narcissist.

When a narcissist likes someone, they would turn on their charm on them and for a brief moment, that person would feel like they are the most special people in the world. In this timeframe, the narcissist would push back gently to get a feel of their resistance level. The weaker it is, the more they push. In this stage, they would continue to maintain their charming façade. And then when they get to a point where they are absolutely certain that this person is enthralled with them, their sadistic nature and their real intentions would start to manifest. The charming exterior that they presented would either disappear completely or be used as a form of sick reward for behavior that they consider good. This relationship pattern would play out until either the narcissist gets tired or the empaths wake up from the spell that was cast over them. In some cases, it usually ends in tragedy. That said, let us look at those characteristics that act as a magnet for narcissists.

A narcissist is drawn to someone who;

- Is very giving emotionally and physically
- Has a tendency to put the needs of other people before their own
- Doesn't stand up to people they care about
- Is not anti-social but not very social either because of their shyness
- Has a very strong sense of loyalty
- Is emotionally sensitive and somewhat fragile
- Is easily moved to act on the emotional needs of others

If you noticed, these are all common traits of empaths.

Why Empaths are Drawn to Narcissists

Why do good girls like bad boys and why do the good guys fall for really bad girls? This is the question that comes to mind when I think of empaths going out with narcissists. But after being in a relationship like this, I understand why I went out with this person. Empaths are people fixers and we are naturally drawn to people that we think new can fix. The narcissist may turn on their charm to the max but on some level, I believe that an empath can always sense the damage underneath. And it is this damage that reels us in. We feed ourselves that we are going to be that special person who fixes them and makes them as right as rain. Every single gesture that is good and right towards us goes on to cement or affirm this illusion we have created and every struggle is interpreted one of the things that we have to tolerate until we hit our goals. If we dwell on this illusion long enough, the lines between reality and fiction become blurred and that illusion becomes a living breathing reality.

The primary attraction in all this for an empath has got to be the damage persona that we sense. And then the next thing would be our need to punish ourselves when we fail at our people projects. Except in this situation, the person meting out the punishment is the narcissistic figure in our lives. I think the last piece in this puzzle would be the fact that empaths feed off emotions and the ego of a narcissist feeds off people who feed off their emotion. This appears to be a symbiotic relationship in the most unhealthy way as one party is being fed with nourishments while the other party is getting toxins.

As an empath reading this, I am sure that you would have recognized a similar pattern of behavior that was exhibited in your previous or current relationship. For those whose previous relationship showed this pattern, be thankful that you dodged a bullet. If you need to talk to a psychologist to help you heal from the damage of that relationship (there will be damages) don't hesitate to speak to someone. Get closure, find yourself again and let it go. If this is your current relationship, it might be time for you to call it quits. This is not a healthy situation for you. If you have not yet been cut off from your friends and family that you trust (this is a classic narcissist move), you need to reach out to someone and ask for an intervention. In the very least, take a temporary break from this person. Don't expect this to happen without some negative reaction from the narcissist because his or her ego would be bruised and they would want to redeem it.

Signs an Empath is with an Emotional Vampire

If you're an outside the observing the relationship dynamics between an empath and a narcissist, it is not difficult to see where the hurt is coming from and where it is going. Narcissist are emotionally draining and yet the empath remains in that relationship anyway. Being an observer of my own past relationships, I can pinpoint the exact moment where I figured things were going terribly wrong. No matter how well a narcissist presents themselves, there are signs even from the beginning. You just have to be open-minded and let go of any illusions you may have. This is the hardest part but we will talk about this in the next segment. For now, let us look at those signs that can tell you immediately that the relationship you are in is destroying you from the inside.

1. You are fighting a solo battle

For starters, you want the growth of the person more than they do. There is a general saying there you can take the horse to the water but you cannot force it to drink. Individual growth is something that we have to desire for ourselves. Now, I get that as an empath, we get to see sides of a person that not many people see because we look inwards as opposed outwards. The problem is that the person we see on the inside is the person who they have a potential to become however we look at that as a reality and we commit ourselves to that illusion. If they can't see what you see, there is nothing that can be done to change things. Recognize this.

2. Everything in your relationship seems to be about them

A relationship is a two-way street. As long as they are 2 people involved, it is important that the needs, opinions, and feelings of the parties involved are recognized an attended too equally. Anything less would mean that one party is benefiting and the other party is suffering. Empaths have a tendency to be addicted to the suffering that is usually self-inflicted. This is difficult enough not to mention unhealthy to deal with on your own but if you are in a relationship and this is what you're going through, chances are you have an emotional vampire in your life who is leeching you for everything that you have. It may be time to check out of that relationship.

3. They have a general sense of entitlement

Just because you are in a relationship with someone doesn't mean that you owe them anything. People get together for mutually beneficial reasons however, there shouldn't be any sense of entitlement as to the fulfillment of those reasons. You are your own person. What you do with your time and how you do it is exactly your business. If anyone tries to force their needs on you, that is a red flag.

4. The arrogance of the person you are dealing with borders on a power play

Some people are generally arrogant we all have our pride and egos. But when a person becomes condescending in their behavior toward you, it becomes unhealthy. You deserve to be respected as a person and a relationship where there is no respect except when you are dealing with the opinions and thoughts of the other person changes from a loving union to a slave and master type situation.

5. Your social life is being controlled by the other person

As empaths, we have our periods of isolation. However, we are not introverts by choice. We always have that circle of friends or family or people that we connect with in general. The narcissist in our lives would work hard in ensuring that we are disconnected from those people that matter to us. For them, having an empath isolated from their social network would make them more malleable to their manipulations. They also feel like there are going to be fewer interruptions this way.

How to Stop Being a Target for Emotional and Energy Vampires

From my experience, the hardest word for an empath to say which coincidentally also happens to be the magic word that can go a long way to making life significantly better for them is the word, no. Apart from the ability to say no to people. I believe that by recognizing these signs which I listed above you are putting yourself on the right track to preventing yourself from getting into toxic relationships. Now that you can spot an abusive relationship, here are a few more things you can do to protect yourself;

1. Educate yourself on the concepts of an ideal relationship

Empires tend to get into their head when it comes to relationship. Like the narcissist, they project their own perception of a relationship. Unfortunately, it is often based on their personal experiences with people. This can be wrong because most times, their relationship with people tend to have this parasitic component where one person feeds off the other person. Healthy relationships don't work that way. Today, I urge you to read up on relationship materials; go on the Internet, read books and pay attention to the healthy couples in your life. Let the things that you discover help guide you to what a healthy and normal relationship is meant to look like.

2. Don't ignore your instincts

One of the wonderful gifts that we have as empaths is the ability to accurately read people, however, when our emotions are involved, we overlook the information our instincts are trying to pass them across to us. We ignore our guts and focus instead on the illusions we have built around the relationship and when this happens, even when we see physical red flags pointing us towards the toxicity of the relationship we still choose to remain. One of the many important things you are going to learn by the time you are done reading this book is that your instinct as an empath is powerful and it is also one of the guiding forces in your life. From this point on, you have to learn to pay attention to what the inner voice is saying.

3. Stop treating people as projects that need to be fixed

When we go into a relationship, we look at a person as a task to score us some mental points if we succeed in fixing them. When a person becomes a project, we fail to see the human element and oftentimes, that human element is the ability to go dark emotionally. Having that kind of mentality often gets us in trouble because when you cease to see a person as an actual person, you would be blinded to their potential to hurt you. You get caught up in the image you have created in your head. Your weakness is your deadly attraction to people who are damaged and emotionally unstable. Recognize this and make efforts to correct it as soon as possible.

4. Get to know a person before you decide to date them

A lot of mistakes can be avoided if you take the time to know the person that you are committing yourself to. They may present a false exterior initially, but with the time you have deliberately created to get to know each other, you can successfully peel off those layers and get to see them for who they really are. This is a Golden rule for every kind of relationship but it is especially important for empaths.

5. Teach yourself to desire the best

Most empaths feel that it is conceited to want or desire good things and this is understandable as it goes against their nature which puts everyone before themselves. But if you want to avoid toxic relationships it is important that not only are you able to recognize good things and good people, you should also capable of wanting those good things for yourself. You deserve happiness. Always remind yourself that no matter how much you give of yourself, you cannot make someone that is by nature bad become good. It is like drinking poison in the hope that by the time the poison gets to your stomach, it will turn into a refreshing drink. It does not make sense.

Chapter Six - Healing the Empath Heart

I am not the kind of person who likes to indulge in self-pity but I think in this place where we are right now, it would only be fair to recognize the emotional struggle that we all go through as empaths. After decompressing everything I did in the last chapter, it just feels like this is the right time to simply put a pause on everything and inhale... breath in the moment. Life really is beautiful. And we can only enjoy it if we can get out of our heads for a moment. Because I am an empath, I understand living outside our heads is not really a luxury we can afford especially since we have to deal with people and their emotions every other day. But that is fine. We need these emotions in other to feed the gift that we have on the inside, however, as we go through these emotions it is important to have a balance where we not only let go of the painful and hurtful things that we feel, we find a way to heal our hearts.

In the first chapter of this book, I talked about some of the misconceptions that people have about empaths. One of those misconceptions is the idea that empaths are broken people. Sometimes the pain that we carry is not our pain. Remember the mirror effect? These are feelings that we absorb from other people and if we don't deal with those feelings, we could end up with a crisis on our hands. What is the point of all of this? Healing in this sense does not necessarily mean that we are broken. Healing for us is a way to sort through the emotions; a way to relax and calm are in ourselves. Healing for an empath is more than just a biological activity brought on by pain. It is a pathway to our balanced emotional well-being.

5 Healing Activities for Empaths to Relax

There are different kinds of empaths (we have looked at more than a handful of them already) and the key to their healing usually lies in their intrinsic nature. For the compassionate empath, their road to healing could probably be found in activities that reward their need to help people. So, something as simple as serving soup in a homeless shelter would be relaxing. For physical empaths, activities that involve connecting with people especially when the focus of the connection is healing would be helpful. Such activities could be either a nice body massage or a Reiki healing session. For animal empaths, just spending a day indulging in a fun activity with their favorite pets can do a lot of wonders for their mental health. These things I have mentioned are unique to the nature of the empath

However, there are simple general activities that empaths can carry out that will bring them to that place where they can start to experience healing internally. If you take anything away from this chapter, let it be the fact that the healing of an empath is not initiated by a drug or the use of a substance no matter how mild. You don't need to start doing something that could become addictive. However, I created a list of 5 general activities that can help you get to a place of calm. Use this as a guide. The goal is that at the end of the segment, you would be able to relate with more than one or two activities on that list. Remember your emotional well-being is very important. If you are going to ever enjoy your gifts as an empath, you need to learn to relax.

1. Start journaling

Journaling is a therapeutic activity that you may not realize you need. It is an excellent way to get you out of your head. If you are observant, you may have noticed that I have used this phrase "get out of your head", a lot. What I mean is getting out of that mental space where you are constantly processing emotions. I know that as an empath you need to deal with different kinds of emotions at the same time. If you keep that process inside your head especially over a long period of time, chances are you're going to end up stressed out. Not many empaths have friends that they can talk to or people who will even understand what they're going through. A Journal enables you to write out your thoughts and sort through your feelings without having to deal with the backlash of processing those various emotions. it is a relaxing experience as it gives you focus and when you have focus, you are more in control of what you feel and how it affects you.

2. Release your inner artist

This part can be a little bit difficult to understand. But this is what I mean. When you are going through one of those emotional experiences, you can take that pain and turn it into art by engaging in activities that require you to be creative. This could be an activity like writing a poem, painting or something like woodwork. Now realize this, it is not about what you create. It is about the process. From experience, this process creates what I call transference of energy. That negative emotion you are feeling is converted into a creative process that has the potential to become an art. You don't have to aspire to do something grand (that would only aggravate the stress), it could be something as simple as splashing colors on a board or playing around with words. These are very cool ways to help you again, get out of your head

3. Champion a cause you care about

You know you want to make a difference and alleviate the sufferings of people. Taking a moment to give towards a cause that is important to you can have a relaxing effect on you. If you prefer to be hands-on, you can volunteer for a few minutes or hours (depending on your schedule). The helps you take care of your "people project" instinct while giving you some appropriate distance.

4. Change your routine

Empaths are creatures of habits. They feel safe in those routines even though those routines may not be good for their mental and physical health in the long run (remember my couch and pastry experience?). Breaking from routine might sound scary but when you take the step, the result can be elating. A word of caution though. Ensure that the new routine you are signing up for is beneficial to your mental health.

5. Meditation

This list would not be complete if there wasn't a mention of meditation. If you learn how to do it right, you can induce a state of complete calm no matter how stressed out you feel. Include words of affirmation as part of your meditation routine to make the meditation experience even more relaxing. I found my peace in Reiki, an energy healing journey that I take daily.

Steps to Heal Your Emotional Triggers

Emotional triggers are events, memories, places or even words that the second you see them, it invokes a specific kind of emotional reaction. When something happens to you, our brains create neural pathways (this is why having new experiences on a regular are good for you) and when those experiences are negative, the emotion that you experienced in that moment is registered and every time something similar happens, you are immediately transported to that moment. This is why you could perceive something like say a fragrance and you are transported to a time in your childhood when someone significant in your life did something while wearing that fragrance. The emotions triggered could be good or bad, this is determined by the experience that you had.

Obviously, you would be comfortable reliving good emotions unless it gets to a point where those memories are stopping you from moving forward with your life. Negative emotions affect us in many ways and those are almost never good. Personally, I think the only good thing that comes from negative experiences are the lessons that they provide. Whatever emotions are being triggered, the fact is that you are being held back from moving on and living your best life now. The best way forward is to do the following;

Empath Survival Guide

1. Stay in the moment

Stop taking a trip down memory lane. If an event occurs that makes you think of the past, don't hold on to it. Focus on what is happening. Don't let the emotions that they bring on hold you down and more importantly, don't look at your present as your opportunity to take revenge on your past. Address the situation as it happens.

2. Don't try to control the situation

Control is an illusion and if you buy into this illusion, you increase the stress and anxiety that comes with reliving emotional triggers. Accept that you cannot control what is happening to you, you cannot control anyone involved in the situation that is messing you up, however, your experience does not have to be determined by this thing that you are going through. It sounds like a contraction but here is what I mean. You have a choice in how you feel because that is what you have control over. The happiness or sadness you feel and how long you feel those things is determined by you. So, leave the situation but control your emotion.

3. Don't run from it

There is a saying that the splash of water you run away from today could become the pool that drowns you tomorrow. It might be painful to confront our feelings. But it is in that confrontation that you will encounter the truth and you already know what they say about the truth and freedom. And this brings us to the next point.

4. Know your truth

Once upon a time, people thought that the world was flat. This stopped them from going on what would have been an amazing adventure and remained where they are because they were caged by this 'reality'. But when some brave scientists were able to disprove this theory, mankind was set free to explore the ends of the earth. Emotional triggers might be based on myths that you have fed yourself and so every time you are confronted by a situation that triggers those emotions, you are trapped in what you feel. Break the cycle by disproving those myths. The outcome may not be something that you like but whatever it is, you get to own your truth.

5. Embrace all of your peculiarities

Life is a fiery bouncy ball of unexpected twists and turns and it could hit us at any time. The people in our lives would come and go. You can't cling on to a memory or a person because you are afraid of what would happen to you after you let them go. This fear is mostly because you haven't come to a place of acceptance. You are unusual, you are unique and the experiences you have are crazy but that is what makes you exceptional. In embracing yourself, lean towards loving yourself more. When you love yourself, every other thing that happens to you is just secondary.

Powerful Techniques for Healing and Self-Protection

The default setting of any person when they feel threatened is to go to a place where they feel safe. You may not always have the luxury of running to your safe space. So, what do you do then? Stop. Take time out and chill. These powerful techniques I have learned have become a coping mechanism for me and I cannot remember a point in my life when I have been happier.

Affirmations

We are made up of the words that we speak to ourselves. If you do not speak to yourself, the words that other people speak to you would become the foundation on which your life is built. And we know that the world can be a cruel place. Some of the negative things that people say to you do not come from a place of malice. They just don't know any better. But regardless of the intentions behind their words, you do not want to leave your peace and sanity to the words of people. Affirmations are words that you speak to charge up your energy and sometimes cancel out the negatives words that people speak towards you. I start my day with the following chant;

"I am a strong powerful component in the universe and I have been empowered to take charge of my day"

Find phrases and positive words that you connect with. Whenever you are feeling overwhelmed by your emotions or the activities going on around you, speak those words and absorb the energy that they give out to you.

Bring Joy into your life

If you have been waiting for that one person whose connection would bring joy into your life, you have been looking in the wrong place. The only person that you need to complete your life is you. You need to stop waiting for some other person's permission to be happy. This is something that you are going to have to deal with by yourself. Empaths are not fond of this truth but trust me, the moment you accept this, you would activate healing in you that is so profound. It would also protect you from falling for just anyone who pops up on your radar. Start doing the things that you love, plan that dream vacation, take that cooking class. Life is too beautiful to spend it waiting. Live your best life now.

Connect with nature

I don't think that there are a lot of things as refreshing as connecting with nature. It revitalizes your soul and leaves you feeling uplifted. A simple walk in the woods can leave you mentally destressed. Surrounding yourself by nature is like entombing yourself in mother earth. This is symbolic of being in the womb which is one of the safest places we have ever known. When you are there, absorb the tranquil energy from what you are surrounded by. If you find yourself by the beach, listen to the sounds of the waves crashing on the shore. Picture your fears and anxiety being broken apart by those waves and let relief wash over you. Accept the blessings and protection energies that you get and believe that you are loved and protected. You would experience a feeling of wholesomeness.

Determine your limits

Empaths struggle with a sense of lack of control. This is the cause of the emotional turmoil that they are always experiencing. It feels as though the world and the events around them happen without their consent. This leaves them in a state of pain, hurt and emotional trauma. To overcome this, it is important to remind yourself daily that everything and anything that happens to you happens with your permission. It is perfectly okay to say no. Put the 'no' out there and let that be your limit. When you feel tired and weary and don't want to go on in terms of dealing with people and their drama, it is okay to say no. Don't let your fear of other people's perception control your reaction. Put your feet down and say no more than you normally would. The essence of this exercise is to empower you and get you to that place where you can embrace the control you have over your life.

Positive Affirmations All Empaths Must Know

With each chapter and segment of this book, I am sure that you got a more intimate knowledge of yourself. Now with that knowledge comes the need to take action. You know what they say, knowledge without action is useless. But before we get to the part where you start acting out the information and wisdom you have received, let us begin that journey by empowering the beautiful person within you. I talked about affirmations before and now we're going to get practical with them. Here are a few affirmations that I feel would be very impactful in the life of an empath

1. I am a beautiful and sensitive soul. My sensitivity is a powerful strength and with this strength, I change my world.

2. I am a very important person, and, in my life, I promise to have people value me as a person. My inner circle is made up of people who value my opinions, my presence, and my feelings.

3. Today I attract blessings and positive energies my way. I reject anything that would infect my world with negativity. My life is beautiful. My experiences are beautiful. My love is beautiful.

4. I have been blessed with the gift to intuitively recognize what is good for me. I listen to my instincts. I trust my instinct and I am protected by my instincts. As long as I listen to my inner voice, I will not come to harm.

5. Today I build a wall around me that protects my energy from people who are emotionally exhausting. I commit myself to staying in relationships that nurture me just as much as I nurture them.

6. I deserve happiness and so today, I will pamper myself. I will treat myself to a healthy diet. I will exercise my mind and body. Today, I am making a commitment to be good to myself.

Chapter Seven - The Healthy, Happy Empath

Now that we have looked at the injured empath as well as the problems that empaths face and then we've gone through this process where we find healing within, how do we know that we have been healed? That is the essence of this chapter. I want us to take a good look at what a happy empath looks like. Because yes, it is possible to be happy and healthy both emotionally and physically. It is always going to take a lot of work. There is no need to hide from that fact. We know that we are built differently than the average person and so the way we react to situations and events in our life is different. Despite the hurdles brought on by our inherent nature, we will find healing. There is no doubt about it but sometimes, the best thing that can motivate you into taking the best course of action for you would be to get a clear vision of yourself. And that is where we are getting to in this chapter. I am not trying to paint a rosy picture. Just in case you haven't noticed, I started this chapter by reiterating some of the difficulties that I feel we would encounter on some level. That said, I think it is time to unveil the person you could become if you stick to the course. Continue in your affirmations and stay healthy both mentally and physically and the result would be rewarding.

The 5 Powerful Lessons Every Empath Must Learn

1. Saying no does not make you a horrible person

When you put an empath in a position with their supposed to say yes or no, instinctively they want to say yes. This is their nature and, in a world, where everything is perfect, this is the right attitude to have. Unfortunately, the world is anything but perfect and so saying yes, every single time you're asked only sets you up for a life of regret. As you evolve on your journey as an empath. This is one of the most critical lessons you would learn. Life does not end when you say no.

As a matter of fact, the opposite is what happens. Your life begins at the end of your no.

2. It is perfectly okay to put yourself first

The empath is generous to a fault. They put the feelings and emotions of others before their own. This nature is what endears them to people but at the same time, it is what destroys them from the inside. On this journey, if you are going to become a better version of yourself, one lesson you must learn is that it is perfectly okay to put yourself first.

3. Your sensitivity is a strength

All your life, you have been told that emotions make a person weak. The fact that you have been sensitive to the things that happen around you has earned you the title of a weak and sensitive person but on this journey, you will discover that your sensitivity is one of your biggest strength. And the more information you acquire about yourself the more powerful you become.

4. You were never the problem

People are going to try and throw your nature in your face. Especially people with whom you have shared some kind of relationships with. Whether it's at work, in school or in your personal relationship. Because of their inability to understand the kind of person you are, it is always going to seem as though you are the problem from the onset. But with the information you get about yourself as you continue to study your personality and understand what empaths are about, you would realize that the problem was never you in the first place. And it is not about allocating the blame. It is about recognizing things for what they really are. Remind yourself constantly (no matter how loud they say otherwise) that the cause of the problem is not you for people's lack of understanding.

5. Happiness is a choice that you make

This here is not something that is unique to just empaths alone a lot of times we fail to realize that the way we feel is actually the only thing that we can control. And yet that is the very thing that we choose to leave in the hands of other people. Happiness is not going to come and knock on your door. It is not going to come in the form of a person who you assume is the perfect one for you. It is not going to be present even if you find that perfect relationship or you suddenly wake up wealthy. Happiness is like waking up every morning and deciding to brush your teeth. It is something that you have to strive for every day and if you take anything away from this particular section of the book, let it be the fact that you are in control of the state of your mind.

Daily Practices of a Healthy Empath

If happiness is something that you have to strive for every day, what then are those things that a happy empath would do to retain their happiness? It is a curious question especially when you consider the fact that happiness means a lot of things to different people. From my personal experience, true happiness does not come from the things that you can own or the things that you can buy. Genuine happiness is found in the little pleasures that you take in the little moments that come to you. It can be very fleeting which is why it is important to be present in every moment because if you miss out on those moments, you wouldn't miss opportunities to be happy. Many of us spend our days procrastinating are happiness. We think that if we are able to get that job if we are able to buy that house; if we finally get to meet that perfect person right now, our lives would be so much better and that is when we know we can finally find happiness. But the thing is that by declaring these words we deprive ourselves of a real shot at happiness. Stop waiting for happiness to happen to you. Use these daily exercises to inject some happiness into your life.

Take a minute to be grateful

One of the reasons that we are unable to find happiness is that we are so focused on the things that we don't have, that we forget about the things that we do have. We place so much value on what we hope to get and pay no attention to the blessings that are already in our lives. No matter how bad a situation is they are little blessings around it. And you can only find those blessings if you make a conscious effort. So, when you wake up in the morning take out a minute of your day to be thankful for all that you have. As they say, you have to develop an attitude of gratitude.

Begin your next adventure

When you get stuck in a rut, your life becomes a very boring place. You lose that sense of wonder which brings some kind of happiness to your life. It is hard to see the good things that you have and appreciate them for what they are and it's not necessarily because you are not thankful. I think it has more to do with the fact that you have lost the lust for life. Today, go on a mini-adventure. It doesn't have to be something grand. It could be something as simple as trying out a new cuisine or maybe starting a new sport. The goal is to bring a sense of newness into your life; to renew your passion for life. When you're passionate about your life, you find happiness in the littlest things.

Show yourself some love

You deserve happiness. I have said this several times and that goes to tell you how important it is. Now showing yourself love is something that many of us kick against instinctively because we think that it creates is a certain perception about us. The fact that we care so much about what other people may think about us more than what we think about ourselves says a lot about our mental state. You don't need to wait for people to love you. As a matter of fact, not many people can love you more than you love yourself. If you want to welcome love into your life, the first place to start from is with you. Show yourself some love. Be kinder to yourself, take out time to pamper yourself. I know they say that going out to eat alone may seem a little depressing. Again, this is the perception of other people. If you want to dine out, I recommend doing it once in a month or so. Take yourself to the finest restaurant you can afford, treat yourself to a lovely meal. Or go to a spa if that is your thing. Enjoy a nice massage. These are little ways you can show yourself, love.

Take a moment to breath

We live very busy lives and the world we are in today moves at a very fast pace. So much so that from the moment you wake up, to the second you put your head down for the day, it seems as though 24 hours just flew by. It is important to take pauses throughout your day. You don't have to do anything significant during those pauses. Something as simple as just focusing on your breathing can do a lot to improve the outcome of your day. When you are feeling tense and wound up, put a pause on whatever it is you are doing. Take a deep breath and exhale; imagine that the tension and stress that you are feeling is flowing out with that breath. There are several breathing exercises that are designed specifically to reduce stress. You could look those up on the internet and maybe try it out. If that sounds a little too complicated for you, just stick to taking pauses during your day. Stop and smell the proverbial roses.

Have a Vision of your future

In very simple terms, this is called dreaming. When you stop dreaming, it is very easy to lose your happiness. That is not to say we should not be rooted in the moment. What I mean is that a vision of your future offers you an alternative that you can walk towards without detaching you from your present. It is important that you recognize the dynamics of this. Going forward, I urge you to dream a little more than you normally would. Picture the happiness that this vision gives you and let it empower your present.

Stop Empathizing with Pain and Start Empathizing with Joy

As empaths, we have a tendency to connect ourselves with pain. When we see someone in pain, we reflect that pain in our lives. This causes us to go through that pain as if it were our own pain. But when it comes to joy or other positive emotions, for some reason we have a detachment. We are unable to reflect that joy and in so doing, we don't live through that joy as if it were our own. Our bias toward pain is not something that is easily understood. Perhaps it is because the pain has an intensity that calls us or maybe the fact that we can be actively involved in resolving some other person's pain. When it comes to joy, on the other hand, it feels as though because there is nothing we can do about it, we don't get involved as much and I think that this is the crux of the problem. When we witness emotions in other people, we are psychologically programmed to react to it and not just react. We want to do something about it.

Well, that was just me speculating, however, science tells us something similar. According to science, our brains do not react with the same intensity to joy as it does to pain. What that means is that as humans, we have an easier time sharing in the pain and suffering of others then we do in sharing their joy. I believe that this experience is even more true for empaths. Experts believe that there is a lot more psychological reward when you are reacting to other people's pain than there is when you react to their joy. This goes on to reinforce my theory that we feel a lot better when we are involved in someone's process and pain allows you more involvement than joy does. When you see a person experiencing joy, you simply have to be happy for that person. But when he comes to pain, our "fixer personality' is put to good use. Now, this does not mean that we want people to be in pain all the time or even at all. It just goes to show what we do subconsciously.

And just because you are programmed to do something subconsciously doesn't mean that your personality has been defined by this. You can take the step to change this attitude. It is good to respond to the pain in other people, but it is also good to respond to their happiness. This is not just for the person you are reacting to but for yourself as well. In order to be a happy, healthy and well-grounded empath, it is important that you strike a balance between these two reactions. When you see someone happy, go ahead and actively rejoice with them. There is no rule that says you cannot do something to celebrate that happiness. If you make the conscious effort to celebrate the happiness of others you would find that there are also rewards involved in this too.

So, today I want you to add to your list of affirmations the desire to celebrate the happiness of other people. When next someone in your circle announces a piece of good news, offer to take them out to celebrate the event. You don't even need to wait until something positive happens. You can just whip out a pen and paper and draft an appreciation letter to your friend, family or loved one the old-fashioned way. Think of a creative way to showcase your empathy for their happiness. It may be a bit of a drag in the beginning, but as you keep at it, it becomes a normal part of you.

Practice Non-Reactive Empathy

Telling an empath to stop reacting to the emotions and energies that they get off other people is like telling them to stop breathing. This is who we are and by now, I am hoping that you have come to that place of acceptance. Now, this segment is about getting you to that place where you don't react to every energy or vibe around you. This can be difficult especially if you're surrounded by people in pain. However, you must bear in mind that to become a happy and healthy empath, this is a skill you are going to have to learn. Look at the things going on around you and develop a different way of reacting to those things. See how I am not telling you to stop reacting? I'm simply saying develop a different form of reaction. To be able to do this, you have to come from a place of self-awareness. Knowing who you are and how certain things make you feel equip you to be more prepared as you can anticipate your reaction.

Another thing you have to understand is that nothing is the way it seems. You may have emotionally walked through that person's shoes but that doesn't mean you have a full picture of what is going on. You see, this is a common mistake that is very peculiar to us as empaths. We feel that our connection to the experience of people gives us access to the whole picture. Let us say, for instance, you stumble across a homeless man on the street. He is holding out his tin cup as usual and asking for any spare change. You immediately react emotionally to his present circumstance and you know how he feels in that moment. But the thing is you only about that specific moment. Bearing this in mind would make it easier for you to develop a different reaction or in the very least reduce your emotional reaction to things.

Scientists tell us that 90% of what we do is based on habit. Therefore, if you want to learn how to develop new ways of doing things, you would have to retrain your brain. To be less reactive, I urge you to consciously take a pause before you react. That pause could make a difference between overreacting and reacting appropriately. One neat trick I had was to pinch myself every time I feel like my emotions are going on overdrive. It acts as a warning signal reminding me to slow down. It took a while for me to get this message but today, I am better for it. I still get affected by the pain that other people feel but I won't dive into everything emotion's first anymore. I feel, I think and then I react.

Chapter Eight - Empathy as a Superpower

Now that we have taken off our rose-tinted glasses, we can see empathy for what it really is. And despite all the challenges and struggles that we go through as empaths, it is safe to say that empathy is a superpower. Empathy is that defining quality that makes us human. The ability to see our fellow human go through life's journey; whether good or bad and have their experiences reflected in our own lives without us having to actually go through those experiences is incredible. As empaths, we set the pace for humanity. We are more than observers in the world's bibliography of anything to do with human experiences. We are participators and, in a way, I would say we are the bookkeepers. It is a cool thing when you think about it. To be that person who witnesses life from the view of the other person. I don't care what people say. They may say that you are too emotional or too reactional or just crazy. We are proud empaths and there is no better time than right now to own the power that comes with the name.

The 7 Natural Gifts that All Empaths Possess

1. Empaths are very creative: The unique perspective given to empaths allow them to see the world in the way that most people don't. This view opens us up to a different dimension of things. In other words, we approach situations from a different angle giving us the unique ability to come up with creative solutions. And even when we are not coming up with innovative solutions, we are very adept at creating exceptional art.

2. Empaths are natural healers: Our connection to the things around us whether people, plants or animals give us a link that makes us natural healers. We have an instinctive understanding of the life energy that flows around us, and we play on this knowledge to provide assistance

to whoever and whatever needs it. Combine this with our biological need to provide care and you have the perfect natural healer.

3. Empaths are alert to dangers in the environment: Thanks again to our connection to the world around us when we enter a room, there something in our subconscious or our being that alerts us immediately we get a sense that there is a threat to our lives in that space. This is not something you can explain. It just happens and it is one of those gifts that we are thankful for.

4. Empaths can spot a lie a mile away: This has got to be my favorite gift as an empath; the ability to spot a lie. It doesn't matter how well-crafted the lie is or how much physical evidence is available to support the lie, the moment an empath encounters a lie, they sense its falseness.

5. Empaths can spot the truth: The same way an empath can spot a lie is the same way they can detect the truth. In our dealings with people, we find them doing their best to mask their true intentions or their true feelings. Our connection to people and our ability to read their energy allows see beneath those layers of pretense and unveil the truth.

6. Empaths get the best experiences: Imagine being able to experience the kaleidoscope of human emotion? That plane of intensity leaves you with a variety of experiences is that not many people would ever have the privilege to experience. The moment we are able to get our feelings under control, we open up the doors to experience life at its best.

7. Empaths are good at reading body language: Communication can either be verbal or nonverbal. Most people are only able to understand communication at a verbal level and even then, their inability to sense the true intentions of people makes it difficult to truly understand the direction of that communication. For empaths, this is hardly a problem. To add to that, they can read the body language of a person to determine what they mean or how they feel

The Best Jobs for Empaths

In my experience, empaths who are self-aware can walk in any field that they put their mind to. It is those who are still struggling with their gifts that find it difficult to function maximally in certain areas. And even then, I feel that this has more to do with their individual personality than their gifts as empaths. Now it is one thing to work in a certain field and it is another thing to thrive in that particular field. For this segment, I am going to focus on career pathways where empath is more likely to utilize their gifts and be successful.

This list is more of a guide so, be careful when applying it to your life. You have to factor in things like your area of specialization, your basic skill sets as well as your talents. Deciding to take a detour into these fields based on your gift as an empath alone is not going to guarantee you the kind of success you desire. The message behind everything I am saying that being an empath would complement the skill sets as well as any other basic requirements for these job roles in their respective industries. With that out of the way, let us explore those job roles.

Psychologist: The empaths ability to listen is one of the things that qualify them for this job. However, it would require an empath who is self-aware to thrive as a psychologist. The reason for this is that empaths in their raw and untrained state tend to react emotionally. Psychologists need a sense of detachment. Even if they can identify with the feelings and emotions that their patient is going through, there still has to be that line for them to be able to offer an objective perspective and as well as creative solutions. Nevertheless, I believe that an empath was born for this job.

Veterinarian: In almost every setting, your local vet is also known as the animal whisperer. They have a way of connecting with the animals under their care and this is not a skill that is learned in any classroom. It is something that is inborn. You need the training in order to provide the right solution, but you need that intuitive ability in order to truly understand the problem.

Artist: It is common knowledge that artists are people with extremely tortured souls and that's because they seem to be sensitive to the world around them. It would make sense to come to this conclusion because it would require you to have a great depth of insight to be able to see things that other people look at as ordinary and transform it into something spectacular. Artists are the reason you can look at a painting and be moved to tears. Or you can listen to a sound and be transported to another universe or you read a set of words and your emotions are stirred. This comes from empathy

Guidance Counselor: This is similar to the psychologist, except this time around, you are helping young people determine their career path and helping kids make the right choices in school. And I feel like this is a role that is very suited to an empath because they can relate to these people like no other person can and also, their intuitive ability to read the true emotions and intentions of people put them in a better position to offer advice when it comes to things like their career or sexual the choices in school among other things.

Lawyer: People without voices need an advocate to speak for them and no person can do this better than someone who is an empath the ability to relate with the situation and the astuteness provided by their training would make them a lethal combination in the courtroom.

How Empaths Can Use Their Gifts to Manifest Success

Empaths are in possession of a lot of gifts that I fell would give them a head start in the workplace their success is not only linked to their career. If applied correctly different areas of your life, you would find yourself thriving. For this segment, I am going to look at five different areas in your life and we would look at how you can use your gift as an empath to get a "leg-up" in that department.

In your career

Regardless of the kind of job that you do, the odds are, you have other people that you work with. For an empath, this gives you the extra advantage because you have an innate understanding of how the relationship dynamics between people work. For you to succeed in the workplace; here is how to work your gifts to your advantage;

1. Use your gift of insight into problems to develop innovative solutions. Your challenge in this regard would be getting your voice heard. Relax, speak your truth and impress your colleagues with your amazing ideas.
2. Use your ability to sense energy to work on timing. This is very helpful when pitching new projects to the boss or lodging a complaint.

In your relationships

For the empath who is yet to understand their personality, their relationships are either complicated or one-sided. With the knowledge you have gained, you can build relationships that are healthy and thrive.

1. Use your gift of separating the truths from the lie, you can actively select the kind of people who you instinctively know to have your best interest at heart. This keeps the energy around you positive
2. Use your creative ability to come up with gift ideas, fun activities and other unique experiences that bond people together and foster friendships

In your finances

Money is tricky for anyone. Empath or not you need basic financial knowledge in order to effectively manage your money. Understandably, money is not a strong motivating force for the empath but there is no reason why you cannot be wealthy. That said, your empathic abilities can help you in the following areas;

1. Monetize your passion. Empaths are moved by the things that they are passionate about. If you can find a way to make your passion a source of income, you would hit a jackpot.
2. Use your network to build net worth. Your relationships are usually your most valuable assets. Grow that and your assets grow.

In your mental health

As much as empaths deal with a lot of emotional problems, if they can also have the best emotional experience. To thrive mentally, do the following;

1. Use your energy radar to filter the kinds of energy you allow into your space. With positive energies, you grow. Negative energies, on the other hand, have a withering effect on you.
2. Use your ability to connect to establish a connection with your true intentions. People walk through life confused about the things that they want. This puts them in a terrible mental state. But not you. Put your mind to it and you can at every point in time know exactly what you want.

In your spiritual life

Your spirituality is not about religion now. But about having harmony in body, mind, and spirit. Empaths are one of the most spiritual beings and you can amplify the experience by doing any of the following

1. Tap into the energy that surrounds nature to revitalize and refresh yourself. This would drain out any of the negative excesses brought into your life and help keep you in a state of bliss
2. Plug your natural talent into your gift of perception. This way, you are connected to a seemingly endless supply of ideas.

People tend to burn out and when they do, they become restless in their quest to regain what they have lost. Your empathic gift can provide a sustainable supply for your talent

The Power of Empathy in the Modern Day

The world that we live in today is chaotic. There is hardly any day that you turn on the news and you would not witness the misery and tragedy that other people are dealing with. The advent of technology has made it possible for media to get to the farthest corners of the earth and bring these tales of woes to your doorstep. With constant exposure to these things, it is not surprising that people have become emotionally detached from the sufferings of people. It has gotten so bad that empathy has become an almost extinct commodity in the human range of emotions.

Today's world is evolving and it is my opinion that without empathy, the world would topple into a chaotic state. Empathy is what creates a balance between the pain that one human is capable of inflicting and the joy that another human is capable of giving. Empathy is what characterizes humanity. We have our differences in experiences, in personalities and in our beliefs. Empathy is the bridge that connects us all. They say that love is a general language and everyone understands it. This was perhaps true a few centuries ago. In the state where the world is right now, love has multiple languages and it takes a level of self-awareness to not just speak it but to speak it fluently.

Empathy is the new universal language. The ability to connect with another being and be interested in their welfare enough to invest in it is what the world needs and this is empathy at the general level. Empathy responds to need and the world is a place that is full of needy people and I don't mean that in the 'clingy' sense. Everyone needs to be heard on some level by someone else. Without empathy, that need would continue to grow for a long time leading to tensions. Today's world is running on the fumes created by these tensions and empathy is the only way to diffuse the situation.

All I am trying to say here is that you are valuable now more than ever. We started this journey with people's perception of empaths. And in retrospect, it would be safe to say that their analogy puts empaths somewhere between an alien and a crazy person. I believe that now you know better. Now you know that you are a sensitive, spiritual being that is full of light and life. The struggles that you have had up to this point are temporary and if you consistently put in the knowledge you have gained here to work, you have the potential to be an extraordinary person. You are the superhero that the world needs in their corner. Your presence is a constant reminder that there is a lot of good in the world and we do not have to look to the skies for angels.

Conclusion

At the start of the book, my goal was to document my journey from being a crazy, out of control empath to this person who is self-aware and rooted in the gifts that I have been given. But with each paragraph, I started picturing your face. As the features of your face became clearer, I started seeing your personality and from your personality, you became a whole person to me. Somewhere along the way, this stopped being my journey. It became our journey and it made me even more excited to share everything that I have learned on my way here with you. People have tried to define us by their own experiences and for the longest time, this has been the yardstick for empaths. We are sensitive, we are emotional, we don't have it together and if like me you imbibed that message, I can imagine how troubled your life must have been up to this point. And this is why I wrote this book. I wanted to reflect the potential that every empath has. We are not reclusive, cry babies but powerful warriors with the ability to change our world. Try that on for size!

We took a lot of detours on this journey and the purpose of it was to look into every aspect of our day to day living. I wanted to break it down into relatable bits. I see this book as a mirror and the clearer it is, the better the vision of yourself that you get. We started off by changing the narrative on who we are and then gradually went into how we deal with everyday situations. We even walked into the dark side of being an empath and to be honest, that was a very difficult process for me. I saw some of the mistakes I have made and that brought back memories of some of the lowest points in my life. I got a very distinct feeling that you had lived through similar pains too. But the good things is that starring into that abyss empowered my decision to be better. Which is why when we moved to the chapters where we talked about our unique abilities. The most intriguing bit for me is the discovery that I actually have the ability to define my life. And this is something that we all share as humans, more so for empaths.

I am hoping that after everything you have read and discovered in this book, that you find the courage to embrace the strength that I know you have on the inside and that you start living your best life now. I can wish from now to the ends of the universe but it is not going to change a thing if you do not believe that you are deserving of this precious gift. Years ago, when I felt that my life was over and I had nothing else to offer, all I wanted was a second chance at life. I wanted a complete do-over. During the years it took me to learn everything I have unloaded in this book; I got my second chance. I just didn't know that 'this' was it. And by 'this', I am referring to the knowledge I had gained over time. My mother used to tell me that knowledge is useless until you put it to action and at first, that was what this information was for me. Until I started making it practical. And so, I am going to pass on that bit of elderly wisdom across to you. Take everything that you have gained from reading this book and apply it. It is in applying it that you would discover what works for you and what doesn't. As you sieve through that process, you become better, wiser and stronger.

This book outlines the process of getting you to a happier and healthier place step by step. I ensured that content is positive, relatable and practical. Being an empath is not an alien concept. This is our reality and part of my objective was to write a book with a balanced perspective on every aspect of our lives. If I wanted to be dramatic, I would say that this book was about tipping the odds in your favor and I believe that we were able to achieve this. In your hands right now a tool that shows your strengths and weaknesses. It highlights your interests and your passions and it clearly outlines your risks and your rewards. It is not a magician's wand that you can simply flick your wrists, say the magic word and transform your life overnight but it puts the power of transformation in your hands.

And now that we have come to the end, it is my earnest desire that your process does not end the second that you close this book. I want the words that are contained in this book to come alive in your heart. I want them to inspire you in moments when you feel down and activate a passion in you that sees you pursuing your dreams to the fullest. However, as an empath, I understand what your biggest struggle in all of this is going to be and with that knowledge, here is my wish for you. I wish that you would see yourself for the wonderful person that you are and ultimately accept this gift that has been given to you. I can almost see the gears in your brain working in unison and I hope that they steer you towards that space where you can finally accept that you are deserving of happiness. That you no longer need to keep putting your needs and your dreams on the back burner for everyone else. You have just as much right as everyone else to be happy. That is not to say that I want you to stop being you…just a friendly reminder that your dreams and aspirations are a part of who you are. On that note, I say welcome to the best days of the rest of your life. Keep being authentic.

www.ingramcontent.com/pod-product-compliance
Lightning Source LLC
Chambersburg PA
CBHW021129080526
44587CB00012B/1205